Grey Stone Hall in Rouses Point was the residence of Albert Chapman. History of Clinton and Franklin Counties, New York, *D. H. Hurd*

First as Plattsburgh National Bank, then National Commercial Bank and Trust Company, and now as Key Bank N.A., we are proud of our part in Clinton County's growth over the last 200 years. We are extremely pleased to be the corporate underwriter for this limited edition publication of "Clinton County: A Pictorial History" of our county's bicentennial.

More than just a historical publication, this book is the story of the people who struggled to make this country a better place in which to live. Their courage, faith and achievements built our county's strong foundation. We dedicate this volume to all of them and their families who will continue to raise this county to even greater heights over the next 200 years.

CLINTON COUNTY
a pictorial history

by The Bicentennial Celebrations Committee

Helen W. Allan
Carol G. Bedore
Allan S. Everest
Mary G. Leggett

The Donning Company/Publishers
Norfolk/Virginia Beach

Copyright © 1988 by The Bicentennial Celebrations Committee
of Clinton County, New York

All rights reserved, including the right to reproduce this work in any
form whatsoever without permission in writing from the publisher,
except for brief passages in connection with a review.
For information, write:

The Donning Company/Publishers
5659 Virginia Beach Boulevard
Norfolk, Virginia 23502

Edited by Valerie von Weich
Richard A. Horwege, Senior Editor
Designed by Sharon Varner Moyer
Library of Congress Cataloging-in-Publication Data:

Clinton County: a pictorial history
by the Bicentennial Celebrations Committee
Helen W. Allan . . . [et al.].—Limited ed.
   p.   cm.
   Bibliography:
   Includes index.
   ISBN 0-89865-640-0

   1. Clinton County (N.Y.)—History—Pictorial works. 2. Clinton
County (N.Y.)—Description and travel—Views. I. Allan, Helen W.
II. Clinton County (N.Y.). Bicentennial Celebrations Committee.
F127.C77C57   1988   88-14991
974.7′54—dc 19   CIP

Printed in the United States of America

CONTENTS

Foreword 6
Preface 7
Acknowledgments 8

I. DISCOVERY AND EARLY SETTLEMENT
Chapter 1:
    Contact to 1815 11

II. THE GROWING YEARS
Chapter 2:
    1815 to 1850 31

III. THE BEGINNING OF MATURITY
Chapter 3:
    1850 to 1870 47

IV. PEACE AND PROSPERITY
Chapter 4:
    1870 to 1880 65
Chapter 5:
    1880 to 1890 79
Chapter 6:
    1890 to 1900 89
Chapter 7:
    1900 to 1910 111

V. WARS AND DEPRESSION
Chapter 8:
    1910 to 1920 137
Chapter 9:
    1920 to 1930 163
Chapter 10:
    1930 to 1940 181
Chapter 11:
    1940 to 1945 193

VI. THE PROMISE OF THE FUTURE
Chapter 12:
    1945 to 1988 199
Bibliography 218
Index 219
About the Authors 223

FOREWORD

The appearance of a new county history is a notable event because it is wonderfully timed to help commemorate the bicentennial of the establishment of Clinton County in 1788. It becomes additionally welcome because it is the first history of the county in one hundred eight years. As only the second history during this long period of time, the citizens of the county have thus had to be satisfied with a written record once in a century.

Those who made this book possible deserve every commendation, both for planning far enough ahead to be able to bring it into print with superb timing, and then for the expenditure of the countless hours required to meet their own deadlines. The director of the Clinton County Historical Association, Helen Allan, served as both editor and author. Her co-authors were Carol Bedore, Allan Everest, and Mary Leggett. Many other persons helped to locate and identify the numerous illustrations that enliven the book and make it an authentic pictorial history.

This publication offers features guaranteed to satisfy every expectation: its chronological treatment, its concise texts as introductions to each chapter, its many evocative illustrations, and its even-handed coverage of all sections of the county. Long needed, this book deserves to grace the shelves of every home in the county, and if the hundred-year frequency continues to hold true, it will be cherished for a long time to come.

John L. Myers,
President,
Clinton County Historical Association

PREFACE

Clinton County is two hundred years old. And before 1788 there were centuries of habitation and control by Indians, French and British. Portraying such a span of time is the daunting but challenging task that we undertook in preparing this pictorial history. If we have succeeded, we trust that we have put together an evocative but coherent story of our county's development from "Forest Frontier to Farm Community," as Philip White subtitles his history of early Beekmantown, and from farm community to the complexities of late twentieth-century suburban development.

    The imagery we have tried to create has been immeasurably aided by a word/picture combination. We have been surprised but pleased to discover the wealth of pictorial collections that have been available to us. So rich are these resources that we have been able to include only a small portion of the total. To cover as large an area as an entire county in one volume, we have had to resort to a procedure called "once over lightly." The shortcomings of this process can be corrected in two ways: a future pursuit of details of the story by interested people, or a supplemental study of the fine town histories that have appeared during the last two decades. Many of these sources are listed in our bibliography.

    In the final selection of pictures, we had to omit many good ones. We hope that we have not thereby created gaps in the story. The latter part of the book is more fully illustrated than the early sections simply because by the mid-nineteenth century the camera had begun to make a pictorial record possible.

    The people who preceded us in Clinton County had their tribulations and triumphs. They plowed the same fields and trod the same streets. We hope that their experiences will bring them closer to all of us and will prove interesting. In any case, pleasant reading!

The Authors

ACKNOWLEDGMENTS

Since the authors had only a very short period of time in which to prepare the manuscript and illustrations for this book, they are especially indebted to the people who helped in so many ways: Kathy Cayea, Glen Cole, Nancy Cowen, Julie Davies, Norma Fountain, Harold Hart, Craig Koste, Tracey LaBarge, Isabelle Latrielle, Stanley Ransom, Kay Rillahan, Julie Robinson, Addie Shields, Harold Smith, Joseph Swinyer, and Richard Ward. Copy photography was done by Blair & Webber. If, inadvertently, someone has not been included in the list, they should be assured of the authors' eternal and heartfelt gratitude.

Section I | Discovery and Early Settlement

This dramatic and popular painting shows Samuel de Champlain, explorer of much of eastern Canada and discoverer of the lake that bears his name. Only two things mar the picture's accuracy: warriors had ceased to wear this kind of armor and there is no known likeness of the actual man. Courtesy of the Clinton County Historical Museum

Samuel de Champlain's Astrolabe

France 1603.   Copper, 5" diameter

Chapter 1

Contact to 1815

What is now Clinton County has been twisted and pummeled into the landscape we know today by eons of successive inland seas and glacial periods. Approximately a billion years ago a slow upheaval began to create the Adirondack Mountains, which are among the most ancient mountains in North America.

Consider the Pleistocene Age. Though the most recent, it included four great glacial periods, each lasting about a half million years. The retreat of the last one was completed a mere ten thousand years ago. They scoured out valleys and ground down mountains, dumped huge deposits of sand and gravel, and left behind numerous lakes and ponds.

The last glacial period created a vast inland sea of salt water covering our county and much more of New York and Vermont. Like the squeezing of soft fruit, its great weight depressed the surface of the earth by five hundred to six hundred feet. Lake Vermont had its outlet southward into the Hudson. From this era come the whale and seal bones found in modern times. (In 1901 a bone was found eleven feet below Bailey Avenue in Plattsburgh, which the state paleontologist identified as seal.) The retreat of this glacier closed the lake's southern outlet. The earth slowly rebounded, opening the outlet to the north and replacing salt with fresh water. Aside from Lake Champlain itself, Clinton County has consequently inherited a rich diversity of mountains, plains, lakes and rivers.

Into this paradise first came the Indians. In successive waves the Algonkians, moving from west to east, arrived in the northeast perhaps eight thousand years ago. Until about A.D. 1300 they reigned supreme. Then came migrations of the warlike Iroquois, who vanquished the earlier tribes by driving them into the hills of Vermont (the Abenaki) or northward to the St. Lawrence Valley. Generations of fierce rivalry followed. What is now Clinton County was no longer safe for permanent settlement by either Algonkians or Mohawks, the most threatening of the Iroquois nations. However, it was suitable for raids and hunting parties. In Plattsburgh Bay a special clay led to a significant pottery-making colony, but it is uncertain how long it lasted or who its inhabitants were.

The next arrivals were the French, thrusting southward from the St. Lawrence Valley. In the summer of 1609 Samuel de Champlain entered the lake, giving it his own name. Accompanied by an Indian war party, he waged a small battle with some Mohawks, probably near Ticonderoga. His voyage made possible the French claim to the entire valley, and it remained a French lake from 1609 to 1759. To make good their claims the French built forts as far south as Ticonderoga. They also parceled out huge seigniories (estates) on both sides of the lake, but the ones in the later-to-be Clinton County were never developed owing to the lack of manpower in French Canada.

Shown here is a fanciful illustration in the 1613 published account of Champlain's voyage of discovery of Lake Champlain. On the left are his Canadian Indian friends, on the right the three Mohawk chiefs being killed by the arquebus, a long-barreled gun never before seen in the Champlain Valley.

Courtesy of the Clinton County Historical Museum

But the French had almost perpetual war on their hands—first the Dutch in Albany and later the English, after they took over New Netherlands in 1664. Both had a claim to the Champlain Valley and a thirst for the western furs that were increasingly being diverted to Montreal rather than to Albany. Four major wars were fought between 1689 and 1763, in which Iroquois helped English and Algonkians aided French. Most of the battles took place farther south, and Clinton County's shores were merely transit points for opposing war parties, with one exception. In 1666, Captain de Chazy and other officers based at Fort St. Anne on Isle La Motte were ambushed and killed on the Little Chazy River by a band of Mohawks. To honor his memory the French gave his name to the Great and Little Chazy rivers, and many years later a new township perpetuated his name even farther.

In the final war the French were forced out of Ticonderoga and Crown Point. While retreating to Canada, their vessel scuttled its equipment, including two brass English cannons which they had previously captured on Lake George. In 1968 the cannons were recovered from the lake's bottom off Cliff Haven; the state, having gained title to them, has placed one in the Clinton County Historical Museum in Plattsburgh.

By the Treaty of Paris in 1763 the whole of Canada, including the Champlain Valley, passed into British hands. But the French left a permanent heritage behind them. Merely by being here, they postponed permanent settlement until after 1763. They also left a tangle of land claims which the British disregarded for the most part. Perhaps the most obvious of all are the place names: the lake, three towns (Champlain, Au Sable, and Chazy), Point au Fer, Point au Roche, Valcour, and others.

During the twelve years of peace before the outbreak of the Revolution, a few settlements appeared along the lake. Some were created by individuals such as Jean La Framboise in Chazy and William Hay in Peru. Others were on colonial grants, usually to veterans of the recent war. William Gilliland, in addition to his large patent in Essex County, obtained lands at the mouth of the Salmon River opposite Valcour Island, and on Cumberland Head. He named the former Janesboro and the latter Charlotteboro after members of his family. He kept the former but lost the Cumberland Head and other property because of questions about his loyalty during the Revolution.

In 1769, the most promising grant was thirty-thousand acres given to Capt. Charles de Fredenburg on both sides of the Saranac River. Even before the arrival of the final papers, he planted a small settlement—Fresburg—at the mouth of the river, while building a dam three miles upstream.

British policy encouraged settlement, but land grants

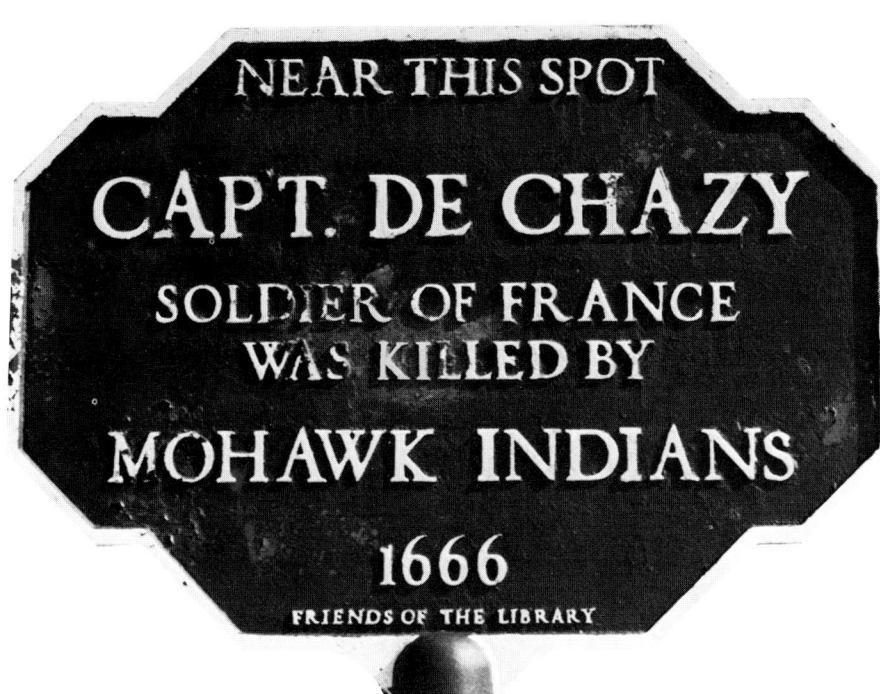

This historical marker was erected near the mouth of the Little Chazy River by the Friends of the Chazy Library. It commemorates the fatal ambush of Captain de Chazy by a war party of Mohawks. Captain de Chazy was stationed at Fort St. Anne on Isle La Motte. Photograph courtesy of the Clinton County Historical Museum.

The French sought to fasten their grip on the Champlain Valley in 1731 with this strategically placed fortress at Crown Point. The French lost it to English General Amherst in 1759, blowing it up before their retreat. The English lost it temporarily to Ethan Allen's men in 1775, and permanently with the peace treaty that ended the Revolution. Courtesy of the Clinton County Historical Museum

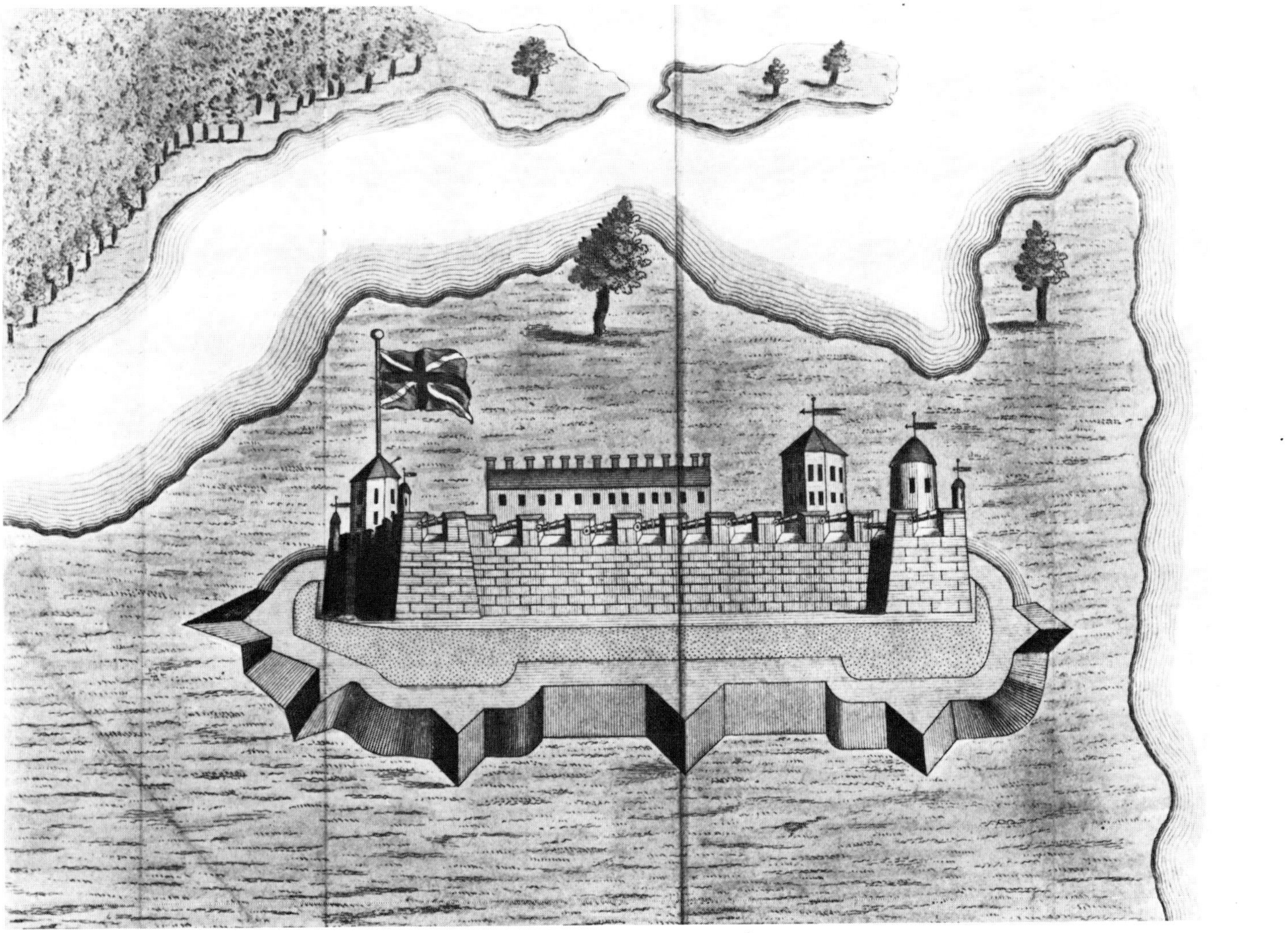

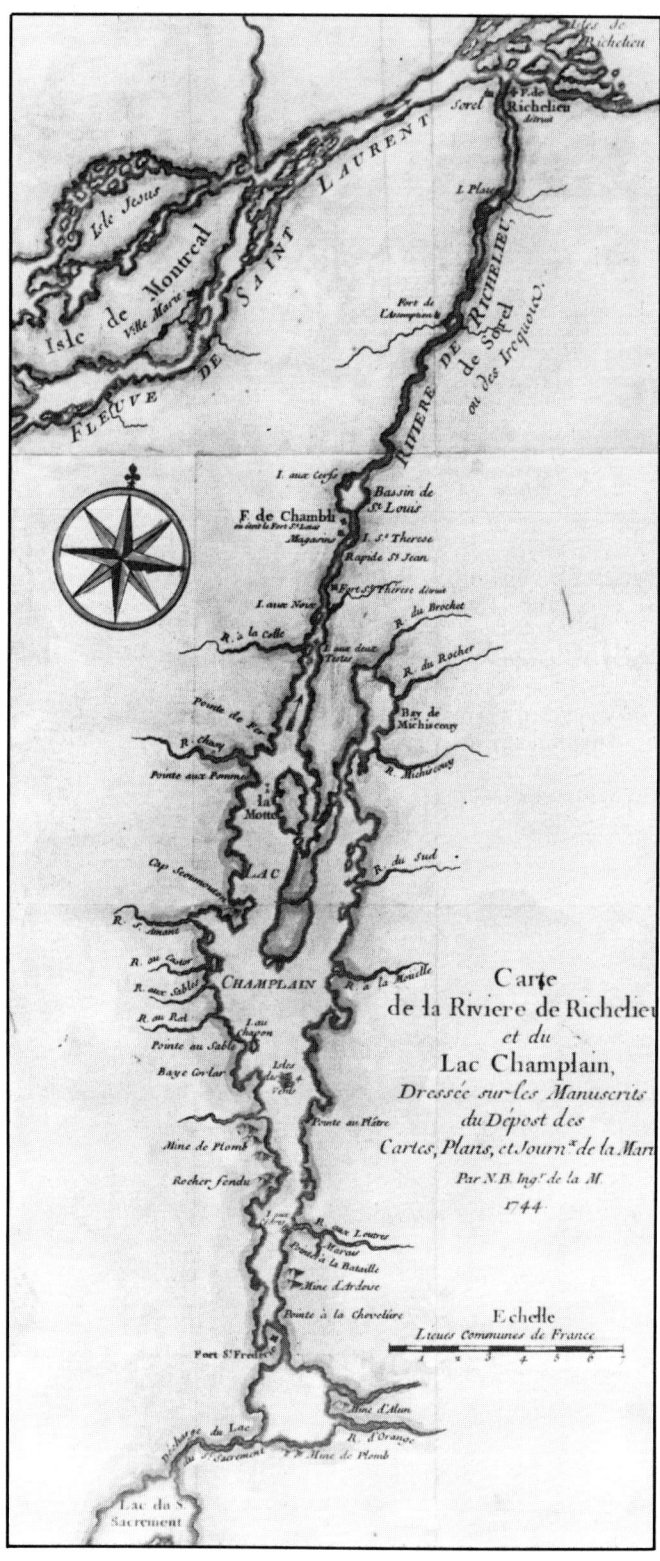

This 1744 French map shows the Richelieu River and Lake Champlain. It was prepared for the Marine Department and is a reminder of how many French names have survived until today. Courtesy of the Clinton County Historical Museum

were limited to one thousand acres per person. Dr. William Beekman of New York City easily circumvented the limitation by obtaining signatures from twenty-nine friends and relatives on his petition for thirty thousand acres. The patent came through in 1769, whereupon he bought out most of the other petitioners and set about attracting settlers. At first he failed, in part because he proposed to be an absentee landlord, recreating a manor after the land pattern of the Hudson Valley.

Elkanah Dean and twenty-nine others, including six Dean relatives, received a grant in 1769, and it occupied a part of what later became Chazy. It was not settled before the Revolution, and only later was divided among the proprietors. It is no accident that large patents were issued in 1769. Sir Henry Moore, governor of New York colony, was an avid grantor because he, as well as several other officials, could collect generous fees. Dr. Beekman, for example, paid him twelve pounds ($60) per one thousand acres, or 360 pounds. The attorney general, the surveyor general, the colonial secretary and others obtained lesser fees, amounting to about 860 pounds ($4,300) altogether.

In the long run the most troublesome distribution of lakeshore property was the British withholding Point au Fer for a military post. A stockade surrounding a large stone structure, known as the White House, served as a staging area for the British throughout the Revolution.

When the American Revolution broke out, war came early to the Champlain Valley with the American capture of Forts Ticonderoga and Crown Point. Settlers with British sympathies such as de Fredenburg departed for Canada. Later in 1775 the American patriots launched a two-pronged invasion of Canada. Although they courted the French with glowing promises, the British had gained their trust by granting them most of what they wanted in the Quebec Act of 1774. Consequently, the American commanders who were authorized to recruit Canadian regiments met with indifferent success. With the onset of smallpox in the American army and the arrival of British reinforcements, the Patriot army, diseased and disorderly, retreated into the lake in June 1776.

A power vacuum was thus created in the valley which the British tried to fill. Their hasty shipbuilding was matched by Benedict Arnold's frantic efforts at Whitehall. The two fleets clashed in the narrow waterway between Valcour Island and the mainland on October 11. Arnold had already achieved his goal of holding up the British until too late in the season for feasible campaigning, but he chose to stand and fight rather than pull back to safety under the guns of Fort Ticonderoga. In the initial clash and the subsequent pursuit, Arnold lost or personally destroyed almost his entire fleet, which would have served the Americans well in the following year.

In that year, 1777, Gen. John Burgoyne entered the valley with a large army and fleet. His exact path on land is uncertain, but there is evidence of a corduroy road across Point au Roche and of some boardings at Cumberland

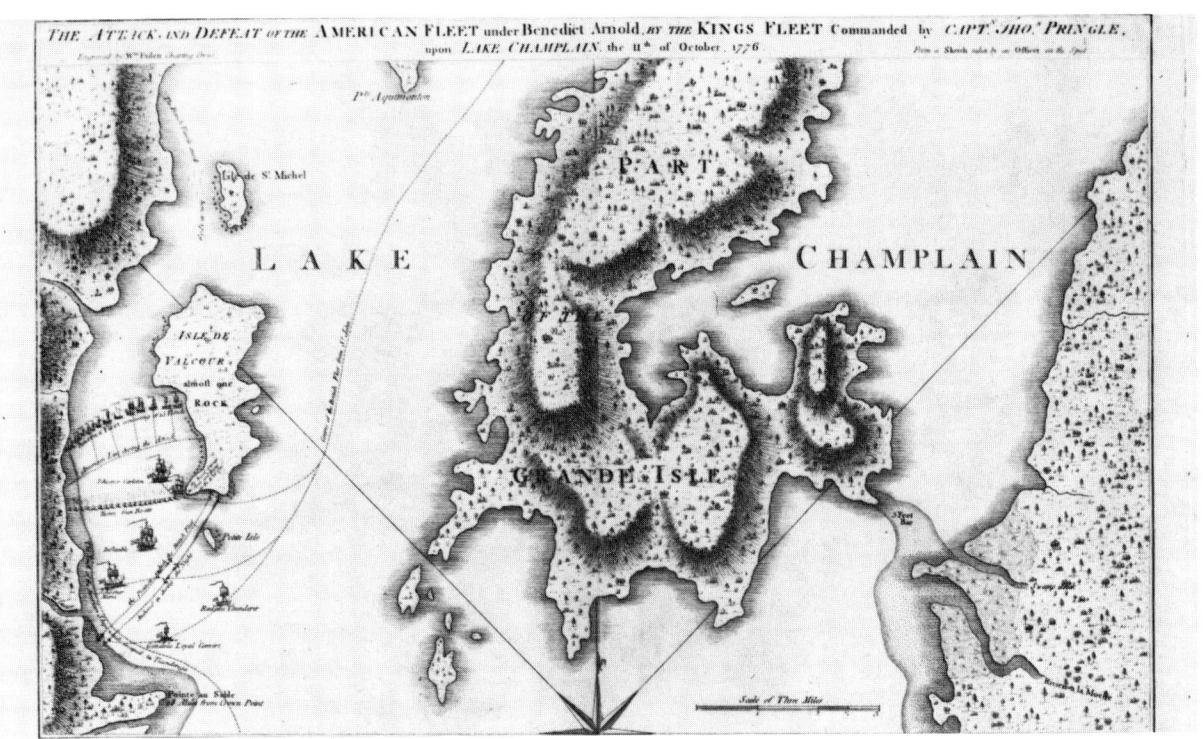

Published in London in December 1776, the Faden map depicts a section of Lake Champlain, which shows the Battle of Valcour, October 11-13, 1776. Courtesy of the Clinton County Historical Museum

The Royal Savage was Arnold's first flagship at the start of the Battle of Valcour. The ship ran aground at the southern tip of the island, and Arnold transferred to the Congress for the rest of the battle. Courtesy of the Clinton County Historical Museum

This portrait of Benedict Arnold was drawn by Du Simitier while Arnold was commandant of Philadelphia from 1779 to 1780. In 1776 Arnold built an American fleet on Lake Champlain at Skenesboro (Whitehall) and Ticonderoga; he then challenged a British fleet under General Carleton and lost most of his ships. Courtesy of the Clinton County Historical Museum

The People Of the STATE of NEW-YORK, By the Grace of GOD, Free and Independent:

TO ALL to whom these Presents shall come, Greeting: KNOW YE, That WE HAVE Given, Granted and Confirmed, and by these Presents, DO Give, Grant and Confirm, unto Zephaniah Platt [illegible] Containing one thousand three hundred and twenty acres

TOGETHER with all and singular the Rights, Hereditaments and Appurtenances to the same belonging, or in any Wise appertaining, *EXCEPTING* and *RESERVING* to ourselves, all Gold and Silver Mines, and five Acres of every Hundred Acres of the said Tract of Land for Highways. To HAVE AND TO HOLD the above described and granted Premises unto the said [illegible]

Heirs and Assigns, as a good and indefeasible Estate of Inheritance, for ever. On CONDITION NEVERTHELESS, That within the Term of seven Years to be computed from the first Day of January next ensuing the Date hereof, there shall be one actual Settlement made on the said Tract of Land hereby granted for every six hundred and forty acres thereof otherwise these our Letters Patent, and the Estate hereby granted, shall cease, determine and become void. IN TESTIMONY WHEREOF, We have caused these our Letters to be made patent, and the Great Seal of our said State to be hereunto affixed. WITNESS Our trusty and well-beloved GEORGE CLINTON, Esquire, Governor of our said State, General and Commander in Chief of all the Militia, and Admiral of the Navy of the same, at our City of New-York, this [illegible] Day of [illegible] in the Year of our *LORD* One Thousand Seven Hundred and Eighty-seven, and in the eleventh Year of our *INDEPENDENCE*.

Approved of by the Commissioners of the Land-Office, and passed the Secretary's Office, the [illegible] Day of [illegible] 1787.

In 1784 Zephaniah Platt and thirty-two other people acquired a state grant of thirty thousand acres of land in the North Country. Charles Platt, brother of Zephaniah, arrived from Poughkeepsie in 1785 and proceeded to establish a settlement. The land grant was given to Zephaniah Platt in 1787, and signed by Gov. George Clinton. Courtesy of the Clinton County Historical Museum

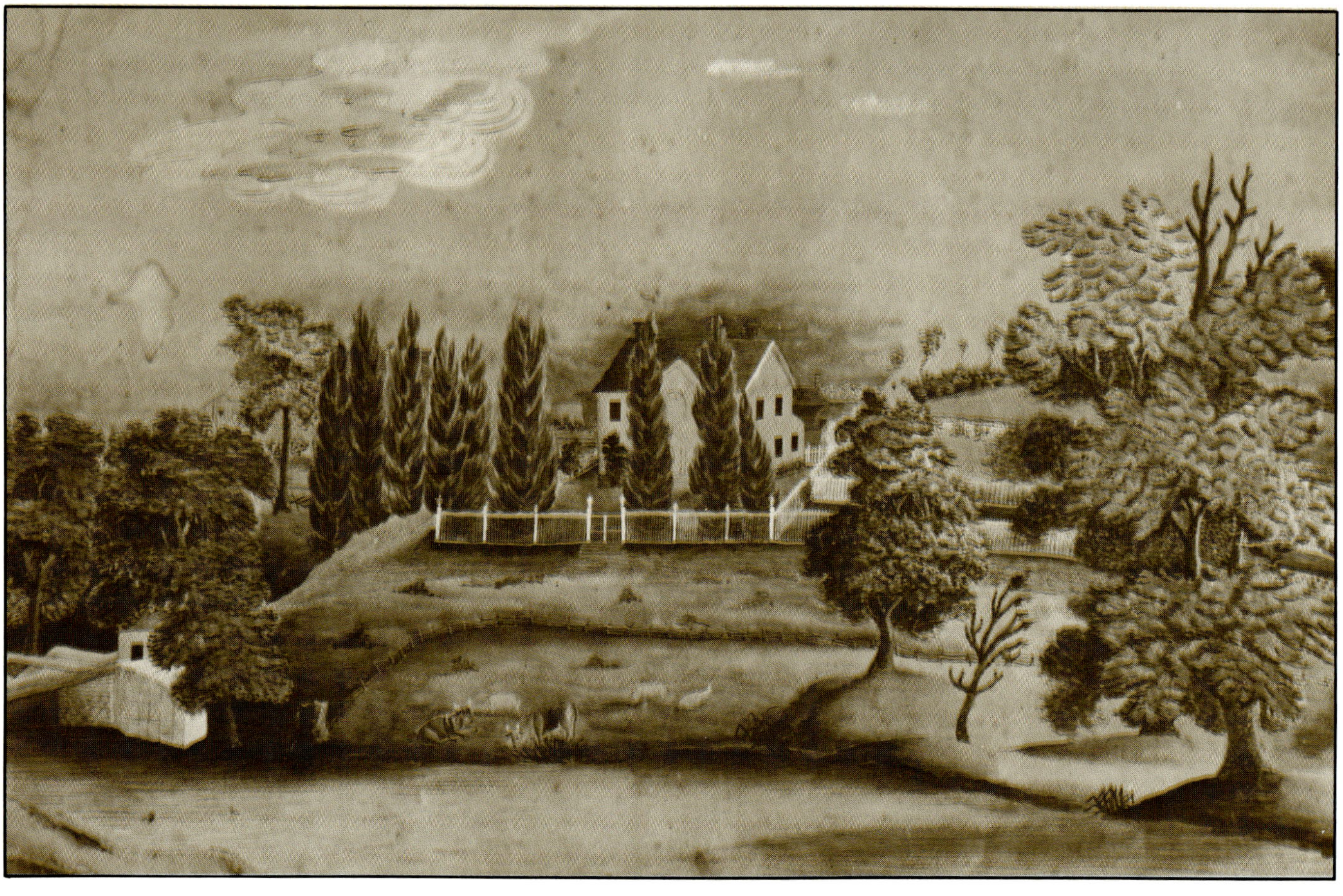

Pliny Moore built this mansion in Champlain in 1800. He imitated some architectural details used earlier in Vermont homes of friends in Addison County. This picture was painted by his son in 1829. The house burned in 1912, but was precisely rebuilt by his architect great-grandson, Hugh McLellan. Courtesy of the Clinton County Historical Museum

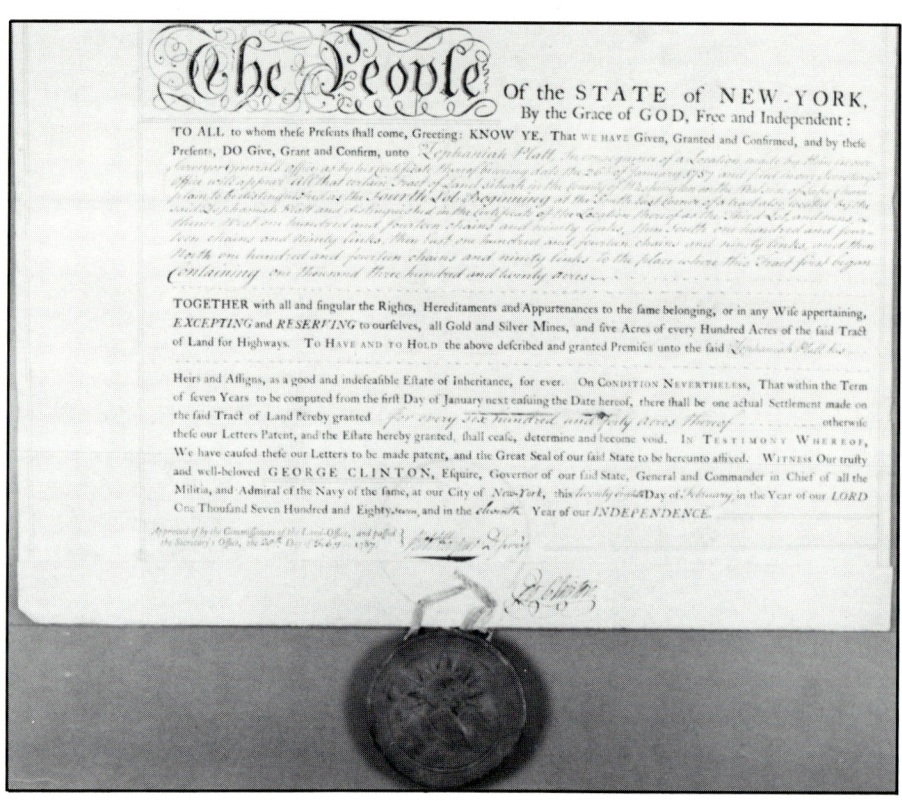

Head. Burgoyne swept all before him in his southward movement including Fort Ticonderoga, until he reached the Hudson River, where two defeats led to his surrender. Nevertheless, Lake Champlain remained a British possession during much of the remainder of the war.

The peace of 1783 heralded a new awakening in the Champlain Valley, manifested by numerous applications for land grants. New York State looked first to its veterans, who were allowed acreage according to their rank. Many were willing to sell to land jobbers, who were thus able to put together large tracts. The state set aside four square townships for veterans, called the Old Military Tract, which included the whole west side of the later county. It embraced most of the later towns of Clinton, Ellenburg, Dannemora, Saranac, and Black Brook. Since no veterans wanted to pioneer so far from the lake, the state revoked the former and created the New Military Tract downstate.

The most successful petitioner was Zephaniah Platt, a prominent Patriot from Dutchess County. He and his colleagues obtained large grants in the later towns of Peru and Au Sable, and smaller ones elsewhere in the county. But his largest coup was the old Fredenburg patent, plus Cumberland Head. The grant was made in 1784 and a settlement at the mouth of the Saranac began the next year. Although Zephaniah did not come for several years, his brothers and other proprietors did; unlike Dr. Beekman, the Platts were on-the-spot promoters who attracted a steady stream of settlers.

Dr. Beekman, as a Patriotic American in the Revolution, managed to hold his lands and, when he became willing to sell plots, was able to obtain settlers. His grant included the later towns of Beekmantown and Dannemora. On the border in the later town of Champlain, Levi Smith, Mark Graves, and others received a grant of 11,600 acres, always known as the Smith and Graves Patent. However, its surveyor, first settler, and principal owner was Pliny Moore. The old tradition that as a drummer boy in the Revolution he coveted the site on one of his campaigns has long been discredited.

The largest single patent that the state granted was the Canadian and Nova Scotia Refugee Tract, which occupied the northeast quarter of the county. It was irregularly shaped because it could occupy only "vacant lands" not already contained in other grants. State officials made a reluctant decision after realizing that Congress was not going to do anything for several hundred refugees from Canada and Nova Scotia. The men of this group had been enlisted by the American army in Canada and, together with their families, had retreated with the Americans in 1776. They fought in their own Canadian regiment throughout the war, and upon demobilization joined their families in refugee camps at Albany and Fishkill. They came to the banks of the Little Chazy in 1786 to draw lots, and some of them established settlements in Rouses Point, Corbeau (later Cooperville), and Chazy Landing. But many wanted to sell some or all of their portion, and thus Benjamin Mooers and Pliny Moore became large landholders. Mooers owned so much land in the later town of Mooers that its founders chose his name as their own.

Settlers arrived in a steady flow, encouraged by proprietors with free, cheap or bargain rates. Moneylenders were happy to help would-be pioneers purchase their farms. The history of rags-to-riches often came true, but the records also contain the sad story of pioneers who lost their property through foreclosure. Settlement usually proceeded from east to west, with areas farthest inland the last to be developed.

Most of the settlers, who came from Vermont, Southern New England, and New York, were content to become independent farmers. For them, after providing shelter for man and animal, the most pressing need was clearing

Timber rafts plied the waters of Lake Champlain almost from the beginning of settlement. Abundant forest resources provided a source of income for many of Clinton County's early residents. Courtesy of the Clinton County Historical Museum

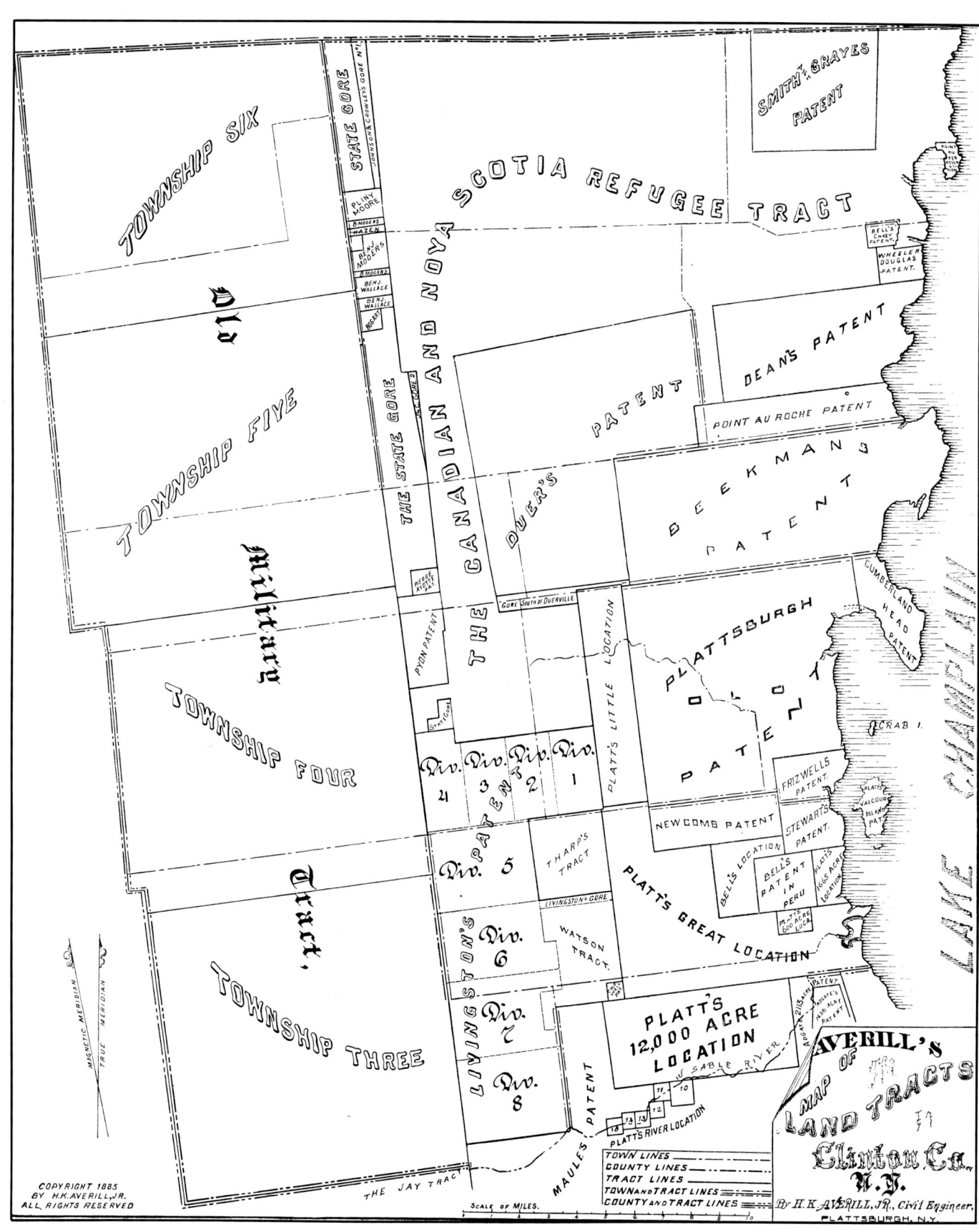

A map shows the shape and extent of the Canadian and Nova Scotia Refugee Tract, irregular due to the necessity of avoiding other land grants already made. It is copyrighted by H. K. Averill, Jr. in his book Geography & History of Clinton County, New York, 1885. *Courtesy of the Clinton County Historical Museum*

THE TOWNS OF CLINTON COUNTY

Town	Settled	Early Settlers	Date of township	Population 1790	Population 1810	Population 1820
1. Altona	1800	Simeon Wood, Daniel Robinson	1857			
2. Au Sable	1787	Edward Everett, John and Jehiel Beardsley, Matthew Adgate	1839			
3. Beekmantown	1783	Benjamin Mooers, Thomas Treadwell	1820			
4. Black Brook	c.1825	Zephaniah Palmer, William Finch	1839			
5. Champlain	1788	Pliny Moore, Samuel Ashmun, Elnathan Rogers, William Beaumont	1788	578	1,210	1,618
Rouses Point	1783	Jacques Rouse, Edward Thurber				
6. Chazy	1790	Nathaniel and John Douglass, Ezra Graves, Lester Sampson	1804		1,466	2,313
Chazy Landing	1783	Jean La Framboise, Joseph Monty, Timothy Sullivan, Matthew Saxe				
7. Clinton	c.1817	Junio Howard, Asa Smith	1845			
8. Dannemora	1836	Phineas Hooker, George Brown, Peter Darouche	1854			
9. Ellenburg	1803	Abner Pomeroy, Lewis Ransom, Aaron Broadwell	1830			
10. Mooers	1796	Joshua Bosworth, Churchill brothers, John Shedden	1804		301	567
11. Peru	c.1792	Jabez Allen, George Heyworth, John Hackstaff, John Cochran	1792		1,923	2,710
The Union	1790	William Keese and family, Peter Hallock				
12. Plattsburgh	1785	Charles Platt, John Addoms, Melancton Woolsey, Kinner Newcomb, Peter Sailly	1785	458	3,102	3,519
13. Saranac	1802	Russell Case, Ezekiel Pierce, Nathaniel Lyon	1824			
14. Schuyler Falls	1794	Ezra Turner, John Roberts, Daniel and Roswell Jones	1848			
Totals				1,036	8,002	12,070
Slavery				(18)	(29)	(2)

This chart presents statistics which make no pretense of naming all of the early settlers. Slavery existed from the start, reaching a high of forty-nine slaves in 1800. From that point it decreased owing to the state law mandating its termination by 1827. Owners manumitted their slaves as the deadline approached. At one time Nathaniel Platt owned nine, Melancton Woolsey owned six, and Charles Platt owned five.

land for a first crop. A skilled woodsman could clear an acre in seven to ten days; he might clear and sow ten acres during the first year if he had nothing more pressing to do. Thus he might spend the rest of his life bringing a sizable farm into cultivation. His earliest cash crop was potash, a by-product of burning his felled trees. In time he might have lumber and wheat to sell. His principal market was in Canada, since Lake Champlain was not connected to the Hudson River until 1823. His shipping was often on huge rafts on the lake, timed to coincide with the spring flood over the rapids of the Richelieu River.

Other settlers established businesses in the villages or on the streams which, when dammed, provided water power for the urgently-needed gristmills, sawmills, tanneries, asheries, and iron forges. The iron age in the county opened in 1806 with the discovery of iron on Arnold Hill in Au Sable. The exploiting of iron deposits subsequently spread along the Au Sable River in the towns of Au Sable and Black Brook, and along the Saranac River at several points in the town of Saranac.

Transportation facilities, especially on the all-important waters of the lake, kept pace with other developments. Beginning in 1790, regular ferry crossings were available from Cumberland Head to Vermont and, irregularly, from Chazy Landing to Isle la Motte. The first steamboat, the *Vermont,* appeared in 1809. Wharves were sufficient at Saxe's (or Chazy) Landing and Cumberland Head for it to stop there, but not until the 1820s did Plattsburgh Village have the necessary facilities.

Neither were roads neglected. In 1793 the Old State Road was completed from Keeseville to the Canadian border, roughly coinciding with modern Route 9. In the same year the Rogers Road from Hallock Hill to Champlain was completed. In 1815 a twice-a-week stagecoach ran from Plattsburgh to Montreal. The area's isolation was rapidly coming to a close.

Some towns developed rival centers of population, and for a while it was uncertain where the town center would be. Chazy Landing, for example, was earlier and for a time larger than the town center; Cumberland Head, with its stores, tavern, and ferry terminal, briefly rivaled the settlement at the mouth of the Saranac; The Union, the Quaker concentration in western Peru, had the town's first tavern and post office. Residents, by going through legal steps, could form villages within a town with their own government. Plattsburgh became a village in 1815; in time Rouses Point, Champlain, Mooers, and Dannemora followed suit. Today they all elect mayors. Another curiosity in town-making resulted from the county line along the Au Sable River, which divided both Keeseville and Au Sable Forks.

Some of the hamlets that developed in the towns bear intriguing names: Jerusalem and Jericho in Altona, Goshen in Peru, Russia in Saranac, Swastica in Black Brook, New Sweden in Au Sable, and Angellville in Mooers. Roads' names also carry historical connotations: Devil's Den Road in Altona, Nigger Hill Road in Altona and Chazy, Shingle Street in Schuyler Falls, and Lost Nation Road in Clinton.

Hannah Kent Platt (1768-1864) was portrayed by William D. Dunlap, itinerant artist, about 1831. Mrs. Platt was the only sister of Chancellor James Kent and Moss Kent of Dutchess County. She came to Cumberland Head with her husband, William Pitt Platt, in 1790. She was blind for the last twenty years of her life. Courtesy of Mr. and Mrs. Wayne H. Byrne

In 1788 there were enough people to warrant creating a new county. Clinton, named for Gov. George Clinton, was taken from Washington County, with Plattsburgh designated the county seat. Clinton originally included the later counties of Essex and Franklin, which were separated from Clinton in 1799 and 1808 respectively. New towns were created in the same way, by being separated from older, larger towns. The first county officials were Judge Charles Platt, Surrogate Theodorus Platt, Clerk Melancton L. Woolsey, Sheriff and Treasurer Benjamin Mooers, and District Attorney John Palmer.

The first generation of settlers, including Charles Platt, lived in log cabins, or dugouts (as the Culvers did in Beekmantown), until they could erect more permanent homes. Grappling with an untamed wilderness, the first-comers had little time for cultivating the arts. Yet in con-

Elias Dewey built a tavern at Champlain about 1800. Situated on a main route to Canada, the tavern was in the path of much skirmishing during the War of 1812. British officers stayed there and held conferences to determine prisoner-of-war treaties in 1814. Dewey's Tavern is one of the buildings in Clinton County most closely connected with the Battle of Plattsburgh. Photograph courtesy of Allan S. Everest

Caleb Leonard's log house (circa 1806) is located on Route 11 west of Rouses Point. Many log houses still exist in the county, concealed by later siding. Courtesy of Allan S. Everest

One of the most striking examples of Georgian Colonial architecture in Clinton County, the Alexander Scott home in Chazy was built about 1810. Features of the house are its Palladian window above a fine doorway with fanlight and sidelights, and quoins on the exterior. The British commander, General Prevost, stayed here before the Battle of Plattsburgh in 1814. Photograph courtesy of Allan S. Everest

structing their homes, they exhibited skill and good taste. The Cape Cod Cottage became the typical farmhouse, while the more pretentious Georgian Colonial satisfied the aspirations of town dwellers. The most historic building still standing is Elias Dewey's tavern from about 1800 in Champlain, which hosted military leaders from both sides in the War of 1812, and where treaties for exchanging prisoners of war were negotiated. The best representation of the Georgian Colonial style is the home built by Alexander Scott about 1810 in Chazy village, with its quoins, fine doorway, and Palladian window. Most of the buildings were of wood but when brickyards opened up, builders such as those in East Beekmantown had a choice. They might also elect to build using fieldstone, as on Hallock Hill in Au Sable and in Chazy village, or from stone dressed for the abortive fort at Rouses Point.

The early settlers, a few with college degrees, were eager to foster educational opportunities for their children. However, for many years they had to be satisfied with fee-paying elementary classes conducted in someone's front room or barn. Secondary education arrived with the opening of the Plattsburgh Academy in 1811 and the Friends' Academy at The Union the following year. Pliny Moore sent his daughters to Montreal for schooling. The few who wanted college usually went to Middlebury, Vermont.

Reflecting their place of origin, the earliest religious sects were mainly Protestant, although the French Catholics in the Refugee Tract held services whenever a priest from Canada came their way. The Quakers at The Union built their first meeting house about 1796. In Plattsburgh the Presbyterians organized in 1792 and obtained their first pastor five years later, but not until 1816 did they dedicate a church. Meanwhile, they met in homes, taverns or the blockhouse. After Bishop Asbury dedicated the Peru Methodist Church in 1811, he came to Plattsburgh and preached in Sperry's Tavern on Broad Street. Other towns followed similar sequences of organizing first and building later. The Methodists were the most successful in meeting the challenge of frontier communities by licensing circuit riders, who could maintain several parishes.

Taverns or inns appeared even earlier than schools and churches in most towns. They catered to travelers' needs, but they were also social centers for the community. Ransom's (ca. 1805) at Chazy Landing had a ballroom on the second floor; Green's (1795) in Plattsburgh hosted town meetings as well as those for the Masons and the Medical Society; Delord's (1797) at The Union included a store and post office; Sperry's (ca. 1800) in Plattsburgh even entertained religious gatherings (It is to be presumed that the bar was closed on such occasions.); and Sampson's (1801) at Ingraham was a well-known landmark for travelers on the State Road.

Other conveniences arrived that also fostered the development of settled community life. In 1797 post offices were established at several points. In 1807 the Clinton County Medical Society was formed in Plattsburgh. Four years later, the county's first newspaper—the *Republican*—was published. Jeffersonian in politics, it reflected the beliefs of the Platts and many other early settlers.

During the 1790s, hostile relations festered between the United States and Great Britain. The proximity of British Canada caused anxiety along the border which was temporarily assuaged by Jay's Treaty of 1794. One of its results was the belated British evacuation of Point au Fer near Rouses Point and Dutchman's Point on North Hero. However, bad relations returned with the new century. To local people it seemed like a dispute over distant and irrelevant issues—impressment of American seamen and search-and-seizure of American ships. To keep from drifting toward war, President Jefferson proclaimed an embargo in 1808 on all commerce with the British. An unpopular order in the Champlain Valley, whose exports found their chief market in Canada, it was widely violated. Federal marshals were unable to stem the flow of goods smuggled northward by land and water. Even during the ensuing war, illegal trade continued.

Clinton County residents' worst fears were realized with the declaration of war in June 1812. However, wartime hardships were unevenly spread because farmers and some businessmen profited from an insatiable demand from the military for their produce. Militia Gen. Benjamin Mooers made the first of many calls on the militia, which caused repeated disruption of lives and crops in the years ahead. Plattsburgh immediately became the point of mobilization for regular and militia units, which were prodded from Washington to knock Montreal out of the war.

Gen. Henry Dearborn arrived to take command of the invasion and bravely marched his men to the border at Champlain. But it was already November, and some of his militia refused to cross the line, a constitutional issue that was not settled until years later. Dearborn brought his army back to Plattsburgh. The militia went home while the two thousand regulars wintered at an unprepared campsite on the south bank of the Saranac. The camp came to be called Pike's Cantonment for its commander, the noted explorer Col. Zebulon Pike. During this dreadful winter, approximately two hundred men died from disease and exposure. The search still goes on today for the exact location of this camp, which could qualify as a national cemetery.

In the following spring Pike and his men were ordered to Lake Ontario. The vacuum left by their departure was soon filled by the British. Having gained control of Lake Champlain, they mounted a large raiding party led by Lt. Col. John Murray, for whom the raid is named. In mid-summer approximately 945 men landed at Plattsburgh, where they pilfered and destroyed the arsenal, blockhouse, several storehouses full of commissary's goods, and Pike's Cantonment, as well as privately-owned property. Leaving there, the raiders destroyed a large warehouse on Cumberland Head and Matthew Saxe's

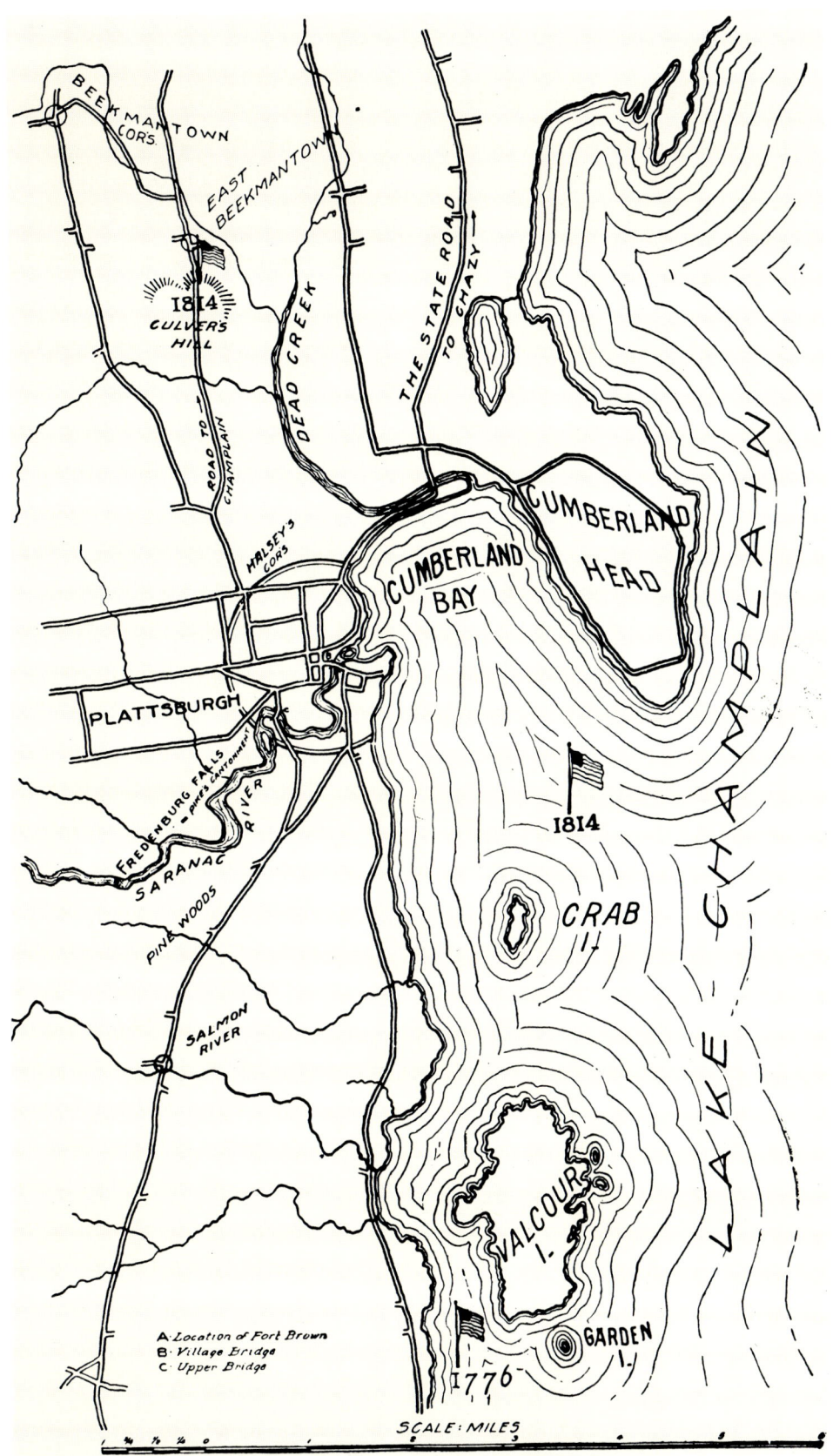

This Plattsburgh area map, made about the time of the War of 1812, is useful for showing the geographical relationship between the battles of Plattsburgh and Valcour. Note the location of Dead Creek's entry into Cumberland Bay at that time. Dead Creek was later named Scomotion Creek. Courtesy of the Clinton County Historical Museum

Lt. Thomas Macdonough (1783-1825) is unflatteringly portrayed in a water color on paper. It is a miniature, painted by the artist George Freeman, probably in 1815. Macdonough was the decisive naval victor in the Battle of Plattsburgh. According to family tradition, Macdonough gave this picture to Betsey Delord, who was frequently his hostess at her home. Courtesy of the Kent-Delord House Museum

This portrait of Lt. Thomas Macdonough was painted by a leading American artist, Gilbert Stuart. Pictured is a copy of the Stuart painting by Thomas Lincoln. Courtesy of State University College at Plattsburgh

store at Chazy Landing. Entering the Great Chazy River, they marched overland to Champlain and burned two blockhouses, the barracks, and a military warehouse. The militia could not be gathered from distant points in time to interfere with any of these activities.

In the fall of 1813 a complicated plan to take Montreal was set in motion. Gen. Wade Hampton was to leave Plattsburgh and meet Gen. James Wilkinson from Sackets Harbor at the mouth of the Chateaugay River near Montreal. As soon as Hampton moved his army into Franklin County, British forces raided Champlain, frightened the inhabitants and caused much property damage. The movements of the two American armies need not be detailed here except to note that the entire campaign was a fiasco. Hampton resigned from the army and embarked at Plattsburgh for a nonstop trip to his home in South Carolina. A discredited Wilkinson was briefly in command of both wrecked armies at Plattsburgh. To reinstate his reputation, he attempted another invasion of Canada early in 1814. He was stopped in his feeble attempt to take a stone mill in Lacolle, and was subsequently court-martialed for his cumulative incompetence.

The capable Gen. George Izard was left in command at Plattsburgh, yet he did not control the lake. In May the British Capt. Daniel Pring brought a flotilla south and attacked points on the Vermont shore, also destroying public stores at Rouses Point. But later in the same month, Lt. Thomas Macdonough emerged from Otter Creek and, with his newly constructed fleet, was supreme on the lake. Late in the summer, in the face of known preparations for a British invasion, Izard and four thousand of his best men received fatuous orders from Washington to proceed to the Niagara front.

Before he departed Izard had started work on Fort Izard on Cumberland Head and Forts Brown, Moreau, and Scott on the peninsula between Saranac River and

Lake just south of Plattsburgh Village. His successor, Gen. Alexander Macomb, continued the work under great pressure because hard on the heels of Izard's departure Gov. Gen. George Prevost crossed the border into Champlain. Prevost led 10,300 men, mostly veterans of the Napoleonic wars. He left 2,100 of them on outpost duty between the border and Plattsburgh so that 8,200 were present for the eventual battle. He spent one night in Chazy, where he made his headquarters in the Hubbell law office. He and his staff lived in the Alexander Scott home, while his officers occupied the Hubbell house.

Prevost made a leisurely march south, which allowed Macomb to finish the forts and to supplement his 1,500 regulars with New York militia and Vermont volunteers, the Vermont governor refusing to let his militia leave the state. Meanwhile Macdonough anchored his fleet inside Plattsburgh Bay, his larger vessels provided with cables and springs that allowed them to be turned during battle. Prevost arrived in Plattsburgh on September 6 and controlled the town north of the Saranac River until September 11. Prevost recalled his army and hastily decamped for Canada the same night.

An exuberant citizenry celebrated Macdonough's part in the victory with a public dinner at Green's Inn, where two gallons of brandy and twenty gallons of wine, as well as cider, port and cigars were consumed. The American victory at Plattsburgh helped to turn the tide at the peace conference which had already been in session for a month in Europe, and a definitive peace treaty was finally hammered out by Christmas Eve.

Peace returned to the North Country; citizens could repair the damages, especially in Plattsburgh and Champlain, and return to the pursuit of their peacetime occupations. The war had two military holdovers that had a lasting effect on Clinton County. A fort was started on the lake at Rouses Point. Work on it was discontinued in 1817 when surveyors discovered that it was being built on the Canadian side of the line—hence the name Fort Blunder. Work was resumed only in the 1840s when a treaty with Great Britain corrected the boundary at Rouses Point in favor of the United States. A second development, in 1815, was the establishment of a permanent army barracks at Plattsburgh, an installation that has continued to the present day.

An engraving of the Battle of Plattsburgh on September 11, 1814, provides an artist's impression of warfare raging on land and water. The British and American fleets fire at close range, while their military counterparts struggle to gain ground and defend their positions on land. Private collection

Gen. Alexander Macomb enjoyed a long and distinguished military career. In 1814 he commanded the victorious American land forces at the Battle of Plattsburgh on September 11, consolidating the naval victory achieved by Commodore Thomas Macdonough. Private collection

The Battle of Plattsburgh, Sept. 11, 1814. Courtesy of the Clinton County Historical Museum

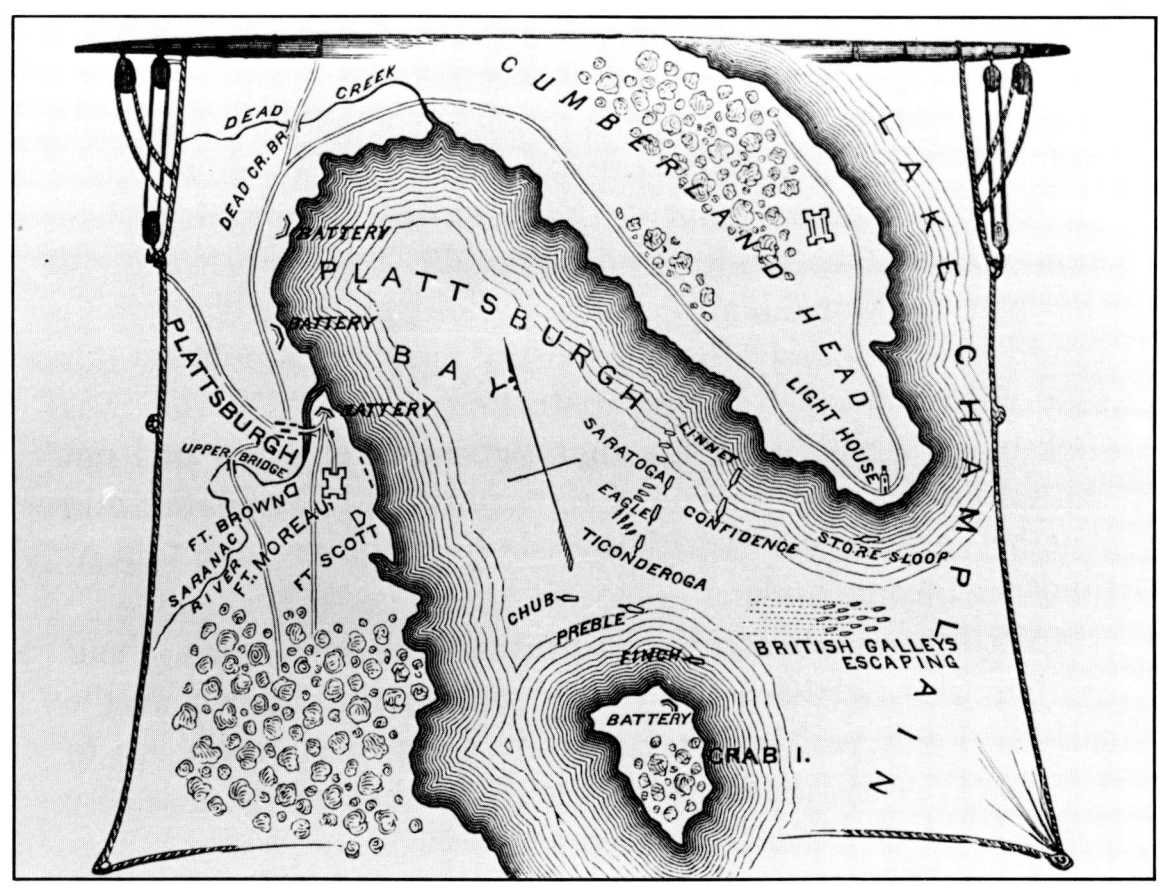

Astride his white horse, Gen. Macomb issues orders during the land battle at the mouth of the Saranac River, Sept. 11, 1814. Courtesy of the Clinton County Historical Museum

Dr. William Beaumont, pioneer physician in research on human digestion, had an office on the corner of Margaret and Bridge streets in Plattsburgh. His book, Experiments and Observations on Gastric Juice, and the Physiology of Digestion, *records the first experiments on a live subject, Alex St. Martin, who had suffered a stomach wound during the War of 1812. This book was a hallmark study of human digestion. Courtesy of the Plattsburgh Public Library*

The Kent-Delord House in Plattsburgh was erected as a small home by William Bailey in 1797 and enlarged by Henry Delord in 1811-12 after he had purchased it in 1810. It is a fine example of Georgian architecture. Delord and his descendants owned it from 1810 to 1913. Today it is an historic house museum, illustrating the furnishings added by three generations of the family. During the British occupation of Plattsburgh in 1814, British officers used it as a headquarters; in their hasty departure they left behind a tea chest, which can still be seen. Courtesy of the Kent-Delord House

Section II: The Growing Years

Samuel F. B. Morse painted this portrait of Jonas Platt (1769-1834) about 1823. From his home in Utica, N.Y. he attained high public office. He sat in each house of the state legislature, was a member of Congress, a justice of the State Supreme Court, and a leading promoter of the Erie canal. Upon retirement he joined the family in the North Country. In 1828 he built a fine mansion on the Lake Shore Road in Peru where his brother, Robert, lived. Courtesy of the Brooklyn Museum

Chapter 2

1815-1850

The thunder and smoke from muskets and cannons were still recent memories for Clinton County residents, but by 1815 they could look forward to peace and prosperity. As the Champlain Valley was settled, the division of land and its uses were of paramount importance. Landowners who had established their claims soon after the Revolutionary War wished to attract potential settlers by extolling the desirable features of the region. Among these was Pliny Moore of Champlain.

Becoming one of the most important persons in the North Country, Judge Moore lobbied for the creation of Clinton County from Washington County in 1788. In correspondence his descriptions included the variety of fish and animals available to fill larders, the arable land that could be farmed, and the friendly Indians who camped along the lake's shores. That these almost paradisiacal natural features might be balanced by hostile weather conditions was a factor less likely to be mentioned by those who wanted others to follow them. Fortunately, there were not many summers like that of 1816 when snow fell in July and the people suffered for lack of a harvest.

Hardiness and perseverance were certainly the traits most desirable in Clinton County's pioneers. Without the benefit of immunization and other types of modern health care, many of the early settlers fell victim to disease, malnutrition or the effects of untreated wounds. Children frequently went to early graves, failing to survive infancy. Excessive childbearing and puerperal fever killed many young mothers. Frances Delord of Plattsburgh lived only a month after her daughter's birth in 1834 despite her family's wealth. Yet these depradations and emigration to the west did not hinder the population's growth. Gradually the land was cleared, farms were established and industries were created through human ingenuity and tenacity.

Trade with Canada was of great importance from the beginning. To meet a demand there for potash and pearlash which could be used in the manufacture of glass and soap, some of the early settlers went into business exporting these products. When clearing their land, farmers had plenty of lumber to reduce to ashes, which could then be sold to an ashery such as the one belonging to Peter Sailly in Plattsburgh. The European demand for potash was so great before 1830 that these commodities offered a major source of income in the Champlain Valley. Lumbering, a major industry in the North Country, resulted in endless exploitation of forest resources and huge timber exports. By 1820 Clinton County was producing millions of pine board feet from its many sawmills on the Saranac River.

Two events dramatically affected the country's timber industry in the early 1820s. One was the Canada Trade Act that placed substantial duties on timber products entering Canada from the United States. The other was the opening of the Champlain Canal linking Whitehall with the Hudson River. The second development had the effect of turning trade in a southerly direction where goods were tariff-free and easily transported, compared to the costs and difficulties faced in traversing the Richelieu Rapids and the northern route to Canada. Boats were now able to carry large amounts of timber advantageously to New York where suppliers could expect better prices. Although the season for boat traffic closed when the lake and canal froze during February and March, the benefits of the new direction on trade were enormous.

Travelers were equally responsive to the possibility of water transportation. Compared to the slow, hazardous and uncomfortable mode of travel to Albany or New York offered by stagecoach lines, a relatively smooth and unimpeded passage by boat was distinctly preferable. Travel accounts in the early 1820s tell of journeys deliberately delayed until they could be made by water. By the mid-1840s steamboat service from Whitehall to St. John or the reverse was available on a daily basis. The great steamboat age on Lake Champlain was underway and the *Vermont, Chateaugay, Andrew Williams, Ticonderoga* and others would ply its waters. By 1840 the steamboat had taken over from sailing ships as the primary mode of transportation for freight through the Valley. Canal boats were also to be major participants in the business of moving freight. Boat owners would keep them working until the ice closed in. Sometimes a fast freeze would catch boats in the canal and there they would stay until a thaw came.

Wharves or landings on Lake Champlain brought business and prosperity to their owners and communities. William Lawrence of Chazy, a tannery owner, built the first wharf in 1801. Matthew Saxe of Chazy was one of those who saw the economic advantages of docking facilities on the lake. Saxe's Landing became the most northerly stop for the first steamer, *Vermont,* built in 1809. From Saxe's Landing freight was shipped north to Champlain in bateaux and inland to Mooers and beyond to Ogdensburg. Other landings were at Cumberland Head where the first customhouse stood, and later at Plattsburgh and Port Jackson where the present-day Valcour Educational Conference Center is located.

Eventually, exhaustion of forest resources caused a decline in timber and potash production, although timber operations on a large scale would make men wealthy for many years to come. Farming, the mainstay of the community, had its ups and downs depending on weather and the availability of loans. The Clinton County Agricultural Society was formed in 1819 in the hope that the organization would promote the county's future in farming. Forty years later, after periods of inactivity, the society established the first fairgrounds in Plattsburgh, just west of SUNY Plattsburgh's heating plant today. Subsequently, the fairgrounds moved to Boynton Avenue in the city. The Clinton County racetrack became well-known in the

This drawing of Peter Sailly (1758-1826) was made by Charles B. J. F. de Saint-Memin about 1806. Sailly was an early settler, first on Cumberland Head (1785) and ten years later in Plattsburgh Village. He became a leader in local affairs, including a seat in Congress and the collector of customs. Courtesy of Miss Sailly Warren

world of racing and breeding.

Many types of farming and breeding of livestock were tried with varying levels of success, including sheep and swine. In the 1840s hay production was important, as could be expected in a region where large numbers of draft animals were used in the lumbering and iron industries, as well as in all forms of transportation. In the early days of Plattsburgh, a farmers' market stood on the site of the present-day Trinity Square adjacent to Plattsburgh City Hall. Formerly a swampy area, it featured a chorus of frogs which provided background music each evening.

Thomas B. Watson, who was born at the Quaker Union, was an early proponent of county agricultural fairs, and favored innovation in farming. Along with others, he pointed out that reliance on home production alone was no longer valid, particularly in cloth manufacturing, which could be produced easily and cheaply in the Massachu-

Mrs. Abigail Hilyard Patchin was sixteen years old when she married Dr. Isaac Patchin of Schuyler Falls. They had fourteen children. This portrait was painted by Asahel Lynde Powers, itinerant artist, who signed and dated it 1840. Courtesy of the Clinton County Historical Museum

Elisha Arnold (1768-1851) was portrayed in 1840 by Asahel Lynde Powers, a well-regarded itinerant artist of his day. Mr. Arnold came to Peru in 1795. Aside from being a large-scale farmer, he served in several public offices. In 1807 he astutely bought four hundred acres of land in Au Sable, which he probably knew contained rich iron deposits. Arnold Hill did indeed produce great quantities of ore. Courtesy of the Clinton County Historical Museum

setts mills. The era of spinning and weaving at home was coming to an end. Fortunately, quilting and other forms of needlework remained popular, and Clinton County's women left behind them many wonderful examples of their skills.

The great fire of 1849 destroyed efforts to establish a library in Plattsburgh, and by mid-century there was still no library in the county. But residents were interested in culture and enthusiastically attended public lectures and musical performances. Theatrical productions usually took the form of farce or melodrama. Between 1820 and the 1840s several itinerant artists traveled through Clinton County, recording likenesses of prominent citizens in return for a small fee and/or bed and board. Artists such as Abraham G.D. Tuthill and Asahel Lynde Powers left behind them a legacy of portraits, as did Ruth and Samuel Shute who would take up temporary residence in a town and advertise for customers. Faces recorded for posterity included Abel and Maria Knapp of Mooers, the Elias Dewey family of Champlain, the Broadwells of Rouses Point, Levi and Eliza Platt of Plattsburgh, and Elisha and Mary Arnold, Quakers of Peru. This was the golden age of portraiture in the North Country which would be followed some years later by an enthusiastic response to a new medium—the photographer's camera.

Newspapers did not take long to make their appearance in the North Country. In Clinton County the *American Monitor* had appeared as early as 1807, but along with others, such as the *Northern Intelligencer*, it did not survive. The *Plattsburgh Republican,* the *Sentinel* and the *Plattsburgh Press* lasted longest and were important channels for political expression. As the nineteenth century wore on, Clinton County residents began to lose their sense of isolation and frontier mentality, particularly after

An unknown artist painted this portrait of William Holt Saxe (1809-1880) in 1834. He was the son of Matthew Saxe, builder of the wharf and store at Chazy (sometimes referred to as Saxe's) Landing. William and his brothers carried on their father's business after his death in 1836. Courtesy of Mr. and Mrs. William Holt Saxe

People and animals were transported across Lake Champlain from an early date. A sidewheel steamship is visible in the distance. Private collection

the opening of the Champlain Canal had linked them to the larger cities in the south. National publications were read eagerly and fashions were quickly copied.

An age-old phenomenon, the building of a community followed by the need to regulate it manifested itself in the beginnings of a temperance society in 1815. Alcohol was seen as a scourge of society, particularly in a lumbering region where taverns existed in great numbers and the consumption of liquor was extremely high. In the late 1830s, spearheaded by the Presbyterian church and supported by the Methodists, the Clinton County Temperance Society was formed. A state organization led by Clinton County native son Chancellor Reuben Walworth already existed. A principal aim was to found a temperance society in each school district. A schoolhouse at Point au Roche was the scene of temperance lectures given by traveling speakers from national and state organizations. The difficulty in passing prohibition in the 1830s may have been due to the addition of beer, wine and cider to the list of banned beverages. However, community awareness was heightened and alcohol abuse did diminish to some extent.

In 1831 Gershom Cook and Charles W. Corning of Troy, New York explored the North Country for the purpose of locating a suitable site for a glassmaking factory. Their final choice was at Redford on the Saranac River where they found the type of sandstone they needed for manufacturing glass. A new road provided a route to the lake and access to national markets, and the surrounding forests seemed to guarantee limitless fuel to keep the factory fires alight.

For the next twenty years the Redford Crown Glass Company produced window glass of extremely high quality, which was used in many different nineteenth century buildings in the United States. The glassblowers also made end-of-the-day pieces from the unused quota of glass, such as bowls, pitchers, wineglasses, and candlesticks, some of them decorated with the traditional lily pad motif. A large collection of these pieces is owned by the Clinton County Historical Museum.

Despite the undisputed quality of Redford glass, the company was never able to secure its financial base. Infusions of new capital and changes of ownership occurred, but the venture was always uncertain. Serious competition developed in Pennsylvania where coal was proving to be an economical alternative to wood for fuel. Overestimation of the demand for window glass, depletion of the forest and difficulties in transportation helped to hasten the day in 1851 when the glasshouse fires were allowed to cool for the last time. But Redford glass remains one of Clinton County's most prized products.

One of Clinton County's most important historical chapters began in 1842 when New York State, perceiving the need for a third prison, appointed Ransom Cook to examine mineral resources in the state and obtain land containing iron mines. Convict labor could be used in mining iron and manufacturing iron products, eliminating

The Redford Crown Glass Company was in existence for only twenty years, (between 1831 and 1851), but during that time it produced window glass of excellent quality, and "end of the day" pieces which are now the delight of collectors. Courtesy of the Clinton County Historical Museum

competition with "free" labor in other types of products. This competition had become a serious bone of contention because prison-made products were sold at much lower prices than those in the free market. Ransom Cook's search for a suitable prison site ended in the remote western section of Clinton County where iron mines were owned by St. John B. L. Skinner, F. L. C. Sailly, and C. W. Averill. Skinner named the place Dannemora after an iron-producing area in Sweden. During the winter of 1844-1845 Cook constructed the first prison buildings using convicts transported from Auburn and Sing Sing. By spring, despite incredible hardships caused by a severe winter, Clinton Prison housed five hundred convicts. Thus began the prison's 143-year growth into New York State's

A "bird's-eye" view of Clinton State Prison shows the wooden stockade fence that surrounded an already large complex of buildings. Despite its uncertain financial status during the nineteenth century, the prison was destined to become New York State's largest maximum-security facility. Courtesy of the Clinton County Historical Museum

Convicts are lined up at Clinton State Prison at Dannemora in 1870, hands on the man in front, ready to march off in lockstep. Courtesy of New York State Dept. of Correctional Services

Convicts wait in line outside the bathhouse at Clinton State Prison at Dannemora. In groups of fifty, prisoners were allowed to bathe once every two weeks. Striped uniforms were worn until 1920 when they were abolished along with the lockstep and other degrading forms of discipline and punishment. Courtesy of Terrance B. Gilroy

On "Soup Day" 552 soup dishes were waiting to be filled and made ready for the convicts at Dannemora who marched by, picked up the soup dishes, and carried them to their cells. Courtesy of Special Collections, Feinberg Library, SUNY, Plattsburgh

largest maximum-security institution and the county's primary employer. Iron mining and the manufacture of iron products, especially nails, did not prove to be economically feasible at Dannemora and those ventures would come to an end in the 1870s. The prison itself had to weather several fiscal storms when its budget was cut and the entire operation was judged unsound. But the intense local lobbying that had helped to bring a prison to Clinton County in the first place carried the day. Clinton Prison was here to stay.

The first churches in Clinton County were predominantly Protestant—specifically Presbyterian and Methodist. Ministers were expected to provide some educational as well as religious teaching for low stipends. As early settler Thomas Tredwell expressed it, until roads and other community needs were provided, religion and education would have to be given lower priority. But churches were gradually established throughout the county. In Plattsburgh the first Presbyterian church housed troops during the War of 1812, but was not finished being built until 1816. The Methodist and Episcopal churches were dedicated in 1831; the Catholic church opened in 1842 at a location near the present City Hall site, to be followed by St. Peter's and St. John's in 1853 and 1867. In 1844 a Universalist Fellowship was organized on Oak Street in a building later acquired by the Jewish synagogue.

Elsewhere in the county churches were springing up. Beekmantown's first house of worship was erected, but not finished, in 1820; prior to its completion people in that area worshipped in Chazy, either in private homes or the schoolhouse. A Presbyterian church was completed in Chazy in 1819. In 1844-1845 a log chapel was built at Cooperville to serve the large Roman Catholic parish extending north and west of Plattsburgh.

Episcopal (Trinity) Church, Margaret Street and Trinity Square, was consecrated in 1831; the rectory was completed 1907. Note the steeple that is no longer on this church. Courtesy of the Clinton County Historical Museum

A rare photograph of the original First Presbyterian Church shows it in an almost rural setting. The church was destroyed by fire in 1867 and was later rebuilt. Courtesy of the Clinton County Historical Museum

Built between 1837 and 1844, the former Methodist church in Rouses Point is an early example of Gothic architecture. Courtesy of the Clinton County Historical Museum

Shown here is the Methodist Episcopal church in Au Sable Forks. Although located in Essex County, it served parishioners in Clinton County. Courtesy of Richard W. Ward

Peru's Methodist Episcopal Church, built in 1811, preceded the First Congregational Church, which was built in 1822. At that time the Methodists were also holding meetings in the village schoolhouse, located near the site of the present Presbyterian Church. Catholic worship in Au Sable Forks followed by 1850.

Keeseville's Methodist Church was followed by the Congregational Church's construction in 1830 and the Baptist Church in 1851. In the Ellenburg area, the Methodists built the first church in 1844. Presbyterian and Baptist houses of worship followed soon after that date.

The Religious Society of Friends, or Quakers, began their association with Clinton County in the late eighteenth century when William Keese and his family moved here from Dutchess County. More Quakers followed them and established the Quaker Union just south of Peru village. For many years The Union was a thriving community, intent on observing the Friends' doctrine which abhorred violence, human bondage or slavery, drunkenness, fancy clothing, class distinctions, and ostentation of any kind. By the 1820s, however, the peaceful life of the Quakers was disturbed by outside influences. In 1828 internal discord in the United States Society of Friends caused a serious split in that organization, and the effects, filtering down to local groups, caused the Peru Union to divide into two dissident factions. By 1850 the once tightly-knit, dedicated community was a shadow of its former self. But individual Quakers continued to heed their consciences. Stephen Keese Smith was an example. In defiance of the 1850 Fugitive Slave Law he took part in

An early engraving of the Plattsburgh area shows a wagon heading west on the route that was later known as the Plank Road. The steeples of the Clinton County Court House, the Methodist Church, Trinity Church and the First Presbyterian Church are visible in the distance. Courtesy of the Clinton County Historical Museum

the underground railroad and hid runaway slaves fleeing to Canada.

Early roads in the North Country were rudimentary, unpaved affairs, passable only in summer when the ground was dry. Plank and corduroy roads were the first efforts to provide a durable surface. But by 1815 a stage route was already in service from Montreal to Plattsburgh and the reverse twice a week. The fare was seven dollars and the journey might take up to twenty-four hours. The distance from Plattsburgh to Dannemora was only seventeen miles, but it could take as long as six hours. Travelers in the 1840s described it as immensely difficult.

In 1817 President James Monroe visited Clinton County on a tour of inspection in the north. A month later it was announced in the *Plattsburgh Republican* that he had ordered improvements on a road from Plattsburgh to Chateaugay, using soldiers of the Sixth Regiment of the U.S. Army. This toll road became known as the Military Turnpike. The road was built in the interest of national defense, but it also provided Clinton County with a serviceable route to the west.

According to David Burr's 1829 map, there were two northerly stagecoach routes from Plattsburgh through the county. They diverged at Beekmantown, one heading west, and the other entering Chazy and continuing to Champlain. Hotels and taverns provided stopping places for coaches which carried mail, baggage, and urgent materials as well as passengers. From the south, coaches traversed a route known as the Great Northern Turnpike which approximated modern Route 9. By 1835 stages were able to reach Albany from Plattsburgh in less than forty-eight hours, although the trip involved great discomfort that made passengers dread the prospect. From a modern perspective it is hard to imagine the slow travel pace and the attendant discomforts in the early nineteenth century. In winter traveling conditions were so hard that only the prospect of a blazing fire and a hearty meal in a modest inn could console half-frozen passengers in an open sleigh.

Two abortive attempts to link Ogdensburg and Rouses Point in the 1820s and 1830s came to nothing. However, in 1836 a bill was passed for railroad construction between Ogdensburg and Lake Champlain. Early in 1845 the Northern Railroad was incorporated and the next five years witnessed the laying of a railroad bed. Although stage coaches continued to run for a few more years, their death knell had been rung with the coming of the "iron horse."

In 1812 the New York State Legislature responded to Gov. George Clinton's 1795 recommendation that the state should establish a common school system. The office of school superintendent for New York was created. Three commissioners and as many as six inspectors were appointed for each town. In each locality trustees were elected to be responsible for choosing a site, building a schoolhouse, and maintaining it and supplying it with fuel. State funds were allocated according to population and had to be matched by the town. These monies were used to pay teachers on a differing scale, depending on their gender. Women were paid considerably less than men despite the equal responsibilities they faced. Women usually taught during the summer term when the older pupils were kept at home to work on the farms; when the winter term commenced, it was thought necessary to appoint a male teacher to handle the older unruly boys. Peru district school records show that a female teacher was paid less than half the salary of a male teacher for the same amount of work. In some towns and villages families were required to board the teacher on a rotating basis. When the "rate bill" or school fees could not be paid, a family might repay the teacher with food and other supplies.

If educational opportunities before 1812 were sparse, most districts tried to remedy the situation according to their means. Enthusiasm for supporting schools with local tax funds waxed and waned according to the economy and size of the harvest, but in general education became increasingly important to North Country residents, especially if state funds were available to help subsidize it. In 1849 a "free school" law was enacted in New York State whereby the cost of maintaining a school was shifted from parents to property owners in general. Negtive reaction caused its repeal in 1851, but a new state mandate increased the amount of public money flowing to school districts. Soon Clinton County would boast a large number of one-room school houses and a new era in education.

An 1836 Clinton County five dollar banknote is no less than a work of art with its various mythological and maritime embellishments. The signatures of president Heman Cady and cashier Phil Yates made it legal tender. Courtesy of the Clinton County Historical Museum

Church spires are obvious in all early renditions of Plattsburgh's skyline. In this 1850s woodcut the gentleman on the right points in the direction of a bridge across the Saranac River at Bridge Street. Courtesy of the Clinton County Historical Museum

42

This picturesque view of Port Jackson on the western shore of Lake Champlain was drawn by Samuel S. Kilburn in 1859. A contemporary description of the extremely rare wood engraving states that "Port Jackson is the outlet to the interior towns of the county. The mineral and agricultural products of this part of the state are shipped hence to Albany and New York, in exchange for the various necessities and luxuries of life. It is a landing place for steamboats, and though small, is an enterprising place. The Green Mountains are seen in the distance." Valcour Conference Center now occupies the site. Courtesy of the Clinton County Historical Museum

A late nineteenth century photograph of the Pliny Moore homestead in Champlain shows a family group. Seated on the porch are Charles McLellan, Jr., his wife Elizabeth Nye McLellan, and their two sons Hugh and Malcolm. The family was descended from early settler Pliny Moore. Built in 1800, the house burned to the ground in 1912 but was rebuilt precisely to the original specifications. The Adirondack rustic chair on the porch escaped the fire and is now in the collections of the county museum. Courtesy of the Clinton County Historical Museum

The portrait of Mrs. Elizabeth Earle Hoag (1769-1856) was painted by the popular artist, Aaron Dean Fletcher of Keeseville in 1843. Mrs Hoag was seventy-three years of age and wore the typical Quaker bonnet. She came to The Union in Peru from Massachusetts via Vermont. As a lifelong Quaker, she always wanted to live in religiously congenial surroundings. She was the mother of eleven children. Courtesy of Mr. & Mrs. George Earle Arnold

Clinton Hall was built in 1850 and destroyed in the fire of 1867 that devastated downtown Plattsburgh. This picture shows Margaret Street before Clinton Street was laid to the immediate left of Clinton Hall. It is one of the earliest known photographs of Plattsburgh. Courtesy of Special Collections, Feinberg Library, SUNY Plattsburgh

Elm trees arched over Oak Street in Plattsburgh until Dutch elm disease destroyed them. Oak Street was named for a huge oak tree that once stood near Broad Street. Courtesy of the Clinton County Historical Museum

Section III: The Beginning of Maturity

One of the earliest photographs of Margaret Street in Plattsburgh provides a glimpse of small-town life in the 1870s. Courtesy of Special Collections, Feinberg Library, SUNY, Plattsburgh

Chapter 3

1850-1870

Mid-century arrived on an upbeat note for Clinton County residents, who were moderately prosperous, in common with the rest of the country, and keenly anticipating the economic developments just ahead. During the 1850s, only two things threatened their peaceful pursuits. One was the slavery controversy, which refused to go away. The other was the depression of 1857, which brought hard times nationwide.

The last of the county's fourteen towns were created with Dannemora in 1854 and Altona in 1857. The county's population growth had slowed, from about 40,000 people in 1850 to only 48,000 in 1870. Plattsburgh (town and village) remained the largest, with 5,600 people at the beginning of this period, while Champlain was second, as it always had been, with just over 5,000. In the ensuing two decades, however, Plattsburgh added almost 2,800 while Champlain gained a mere thirteen people.

The county was governed by a board of supervisors made up of supervisors in each town. Within the towns, incorporated villages were run by a mayor and board of trustees. Clinton County had its own assemblyman, but it had to share a state senator with Essex and Warren counties. Its congressman was also elected by three counties, which were shuffled according to the latest census figures. The county officers, all elective, have a modern flavor—clerk, treasurer, sheriff, judge, and district attorney.

Plattsburgh village was still reeling from a double calamity in 1849. Most of its downtown section was consumed in a great fire, while a cholera epidemic terrorized the inhabitants for a second time. In 1867 fire struck again, devastating almost the same area as before. In the reconstruction, building codes were imposed for the first time that required mercantile establishments to erect firewalls between buildings. In 1864 the widely-known Macdonough House in Plattsburgh burned to the ground, but it was rebuilt by the proprietor's son, and became the equally-renowned Fouquet House. Most firefighting there and throughout the county was handled by volunteer companies.

Most people in the county were engaged in agriculture. Self-sufficient farming had been replaced by cash crops almost entirely. A good deal of milk was sold locally, but the lack of refrigerated transportation prevented its sale far afield. Consequently, much of it was made into butter (more than a million pounds a year) and cheese (more than 23,000 pounds) by the early 1870s. Aside from the usual grains, farmers produced large quantities of apples, especially in Peru and Beekmantown. Potatoes had also become a leading product, paced by Saranac, Peru and Schuyler Falls. Sheep were claiming a final popularity before they, like wheat, moved westward. (The leaders in sheep-raising were Beekmantown and Chazy.) Maple sugar poured from Chazy in huge quantities (it was a popular substitute for cane

This is one of the earliest known photographs of Dannemora Village. A pleasure wagon is parked in front of the post office and in the background is the Dannemora House—a hotel, circa 1870. Courtesy of the Clinton County Historical Museum

The landscape of downtown Plattsburgh was irrevocably changed by the devastating fire of 1867. Courtesy of the Clinton County Historical Museum

sugar), while more than 30,000 pounds of honey were made, with Peru far in the lead. It is worth noting that about 1,900 steers and oxen were still in use, compared to some 7,700 horses.

While the farmers enjoyed a modest prosperity, these were the boom years on the county's great rivers. On the Au Sable it was iron and its products. Industries extended from Birmingham Falls, (the later Chasm Falls) to Keeseville, Clintonville, New Sweden, Black Brook, and Au Sable Forks. The old Peru Iron Company, organized in 1824, was reorganized in 1865 as the Peru Steel and Iron Company. It controlled all of Arnold Hill's output, half of Palmer Hill's, and the complex industrial establishments at Clintonville and New Sweden, just to the west. The industry was originally spurred by the Port Kent and Hopkinton Turnpike, later by the Au Sable Plank Road from Clintonville to Au Sable Forks, and finally by a railroad from Plattsburgh to Peru and Clintonville, which was eventually extended to Au Sable Forks. One station on this line was Ferrona, at the foot of the mines on Arnold Hill.

In their heyday Clintonville and New Sweden were centers of substantial population, with dams and even a canal to furnish power for their many forges. Daniel Dodge started producing machine-made nails at Keeseville in 1852, while twelve years later Rufus Prescott started a long-lived furniture-making operation there. Meanwhile, J. and J. Rogers Company had started an iron works at Au Sable Forks, supplied by iron from Black Brook and half of Palmer Hill. However, the end of these thriving years was in sight. A great freshet in 1856 devastated the whole valley, and New Sweden never recovered. The depression of 1857, with the collapse of iron prices and the advent of cheaper iron from the West, brought the Peru Company to its knees by 1870, and it later went into bankruptcy. The Rogers Company survived by shifting from iron to paper-making.

The iron industry in the Saranac Valley had a somewhat longer life; at the end of this period it was still thriving, although it had its ups and downs during its operation from 1826 to 1892. During its prime years it created many communities with forges, all in the town of Saranac, although some of them are now ghost towns—Clayburgh, Moffitsville, Petersburgh, Redford, Russia, Saranac, and Williamsburgh. The Redford glass plant's closing in 1851 was not a severe shock because of new opportunities in iron. Charcoal became a significant product because it was needed as fuel for Catalan forges.

The relative isolation of the upper valley ended in 1849 when the Saranac Plank Road was completed from Plattsburgh, which was ultimately extended to Clayburgh. Plattsburgh benefited from this improvement because its merchants became the processors and shippers of most of the valley's production. Among the kings of the iron era were Edmund Pickett (Pickett's Corners), Shepard Bowen, Andrew Williams, James H. Signor, and Moss Kent Platt. Some of them lived primarily in Plattsburgh, others retired there and built large mansions.

The Fouquet House was located at the corner of Bridge and Macdonough streets in Plattsburgh. It was built after its predecessor on the site, the Macdonough House, burned in 1864. In the twentieth century it has been a business building, minus its third story and verandas. Courtesy of the Clinton County Historical Museum

A photograph by Seneca Ray Stoddard of the Fouquet House lobby shows a very early glimpse of the hotel's interior. Located directly across the street from the Delaware and Hudson Railroad Station, it served travelers and visiting dignitaries. Courtesy of Special Collections, Feinberg Library, SUNY Plattsburgh

Maple Grove Creamery at Ellenburg Center was evidently a bustling location in Clinton County's dairy industry.

Courtesy of Special Collections, Feinberg Library, SUNY, Plattsburgh

Farmers in Cadyville are loading potatoes to take to the starch factories in Peru or Chazy. Courtesy of Special Collections, Feinberg Library, SUNY Plattsburgh

But the Saranac Valley offered a second option because the river rose in the heart of the Adirondacks. The state declared it a public highway in 1846, meaning that all were free to use it, and the would-be lumber barons were not slow to see their advantage. The Saranac Lakes region came into the hands of lumbermen whose chief outlet was the Saranac River. All winter, logs were cut into thirteen-foot lengths, the Saranac standard, and stacked along waterways. In the spring great log drives were started down the river. They were tumultuous and often dangerous affairs, especially when logjams occurred at such places as the high falls at Moffitsville. Experts were called in who were skillful enough to release the cork log, and thus the jam, and then to get out of the way. With a good flow, logs could travel at about two miles an hour. Most of the traffic was in soft wood, but the hard varieties didn't float readily. From Cadyville to the lake, numerous sawmills sprang up whose sawdust was dumped into the river and eventually found its way into the lake.

Rivalry was fierce, and every gambit was used to outwit an opponent. The so-called lumber king, Christopher Norton, was elected state senator in 1869 and tried unsuccessfully to get a bill passed that would give him a monopoly on the river. Other "barons" were H. Tefft, O. A. Tefft, E. C. Baker, and Loren Ellis. Like the iron magnates, some of them lived or spent their money in Plattsburgh.

A small iron development was located in Altona, and the hamlet of Irona grew up around it. Iron was not mined locally, and at first it was brought in from as far away as Port Henry and Arnold Hill. Its four-fire forge used about three thousand tons of ore a year.

The towns' inhabitants outside the great valleys developed their lake front or streams intensively. The revolution from water to steam power had not fully reached the North Country, and numerous small industries dotted the streams. The most common were lumber and grist mills, while tanneries and cheese factories were to be found in several towns. The more populated centers developed banking facilities, especially after the passage of the National Banking Act of 1863. Prior to that time Plattsburgh had seen the rise and collapse of five state-chartered banks.

The 1850s were the short-lived era of plank roads, brief because the tolls did not enrich investors, who were constantly called on for expensive repairs. A few of these roads have been mentioned in connection with the iron industry. Otherwise, no major new highways were built, but the existing ones were maintained well enough that stagecoaches could keep regular schedules from Plattsburgh to Montreal, Ogdensburg, and Albany. Taverns still provided accommodations for travelers.

The Champlain Transportation Company operated most of the steamships on the lake. In 1848 the company instituted a trip each way from Whitehall to St. John; four years later it changed the northern terminal to Rouses Point. In 1842 Charles Dickens traveled the length of the lake on the *Burlington,* which he called "a perfectly exquisite achievement of neatness, elegance, and order." After that date the boats were even more luxurious, faster, and safer, a promise not always kept in view of the disastrous fires and wrecks that continued to plague the vessels. These were primarily passenger steamers, particularly beneficial to North Country residents who did not have rail connection to the south. Familiar names on the lake were the *Ethan Allen, United States, Boston, Canada, Montreal,* and *Adirondack.*

Slowly the railroad penetrated Clinton County. The first was the Great Northern. Originally conceived by Boston merchants as a *covered* line connecting Boston and Ogdensburg, it was viewed as a way of luring some of the Great Lakes traffic away from the Erie Canal. Long in the

Altona was the station where the trains took on water for their engines. Here is Engine 863 loading its water tank. Courtesy of the Clinton County Historical Museum

planning stages, it occasioned great rivalry among advocates of various routes, including both the Au Sable and Saranac Valleys. Plattsburgh merchants dreamed of making their town the lake terminal by ferrying railroad cars on flatboats, and they invested substantially in the project.

However, when it opened in 1850, it had Rouses Point as its lake terminal; from there the tracks veered south to Irona and Forest in Altona, then north to Mooers and westward to Ogdensburg. The road was profitable, although its early strap-rails sometimes caused dismay. A thin strip of iron was nailed to the wooden rail; because of the car's weight, the strip would occasionally come loose, curl, and pierce the bottom of the car. Solid metal rails later solved this problem. Aside from the convenience of being able to ship their produce, many farmers along the right of way were paid to stack wood at convenient stopping places for the engine to take on its only source of fuel.

Not to be left out of the railroad scramble altogether, Plattsburgh businessmen backed the construction of a line north to East Beekmantown and West Chazy to connect with the Great Northern at Mooers Junction. This line, completed in 1852, was soon connected with a Canadian line leading to Montreal. On the strength of this outlet, plus the expectation that a railroad to Albany would shortly be realized, the Plattsburgh and Montreal Railroad built a spur to Peru and Clintonville. The much-desired line to Albany was still some years in the future, however.

Secondary schools multiplied, particularly after the Civil War when state aid became more generous for public schools; the older academies either closed or went public. Higher education was still not available in the county. Public libraries were developed only late in the century. Plattsburgh had one earlier, but it was entirely consumed in the fire of 1849. Rouses Point, Champlain, and Peru published a series of short-lived newspapers. After several had come and gone in Plattsburgh, the *Sentinel* appeared as a Republican paper and enjoyed a seventy-five year run, while the *Republican* continued its Democratic affinities. Semi-professional theatrical performances began in Plattsburgh during the 1850s, with church facilities, the Academy, and the Court House being pressed into service. Photography began to meet the popular demand for portraits, but only one of the earlier group of skilled itinerant painters remained at work locally. He was Aaron Dean Fletcher of Keeseville, whose last dated portrait—Mary Broadwell of Morrisonville— was painted in 1862.

Clinton County builders had become accustomed to fast-changing architectural styles. Having flirted at length with the Greek Revival, and briefly with the Roman Revival, they now found it necessary to learn four new styles in rapid succession. Imitating the trendsetters downstate from the late 1830s to the mid-1860s, they built in the gothic mode, with its distinguishing pointed-arch windows and doors. In the 1850s came the Italianate in several forms, depending upon the Italian area of origin. A

This portrait of the young Mary Broadwell of Morrisonville was painted by Aaron Dean Fletcher of Keeseville in 1862. He was the last of the competent itinerant painters who operated in Clinton County. Courtesy of Mrs. Andrew Broadwell

modified bell tower was sometimes used, but the most common was the Venetian villa with its nearly flat roof and a cupola. The mansard, an import from France, arrived in the North Country during the 1860s. It featured a two-pitched roof, the lower one very steep and punctuated by dormers. The late 1860s saw the beginning of High Victorian buildings. They were huge, planned to please the nouveau riche, and designed to combine elements of every style that had preceded them.

At mid-century North Country residents showed increased curiosity about their past. Peter Sailly Palmer of Plattsburgh catered to this interest by publishing a history of Lake Champlain in 1853. J.H. French's *Gazetteer of New York State,* which appeared in 1860, may have stimulated further interest in local history. Palmer continued his writing, while Winslow C. Watson of Port Kent produced a remarkable history of Essex County in 1869 and, two years later, a history of Lake Champlain and the Adirondacks.

The dark cloud of sectional controversy was temporarily dissipated by the Compromise of 1850. But the differences between North and South, especially over slavery, proved too deep for a patchwork solution. Clinton County residents were reminded almost daily of the

Franklin C. Palmer of Plattsburgh is seen in his full regalia as a colonel during the Civil War. His military career began as captain of the Plattsburgh Volunteers in 1861. Surviving the war, he returned to Clinton County and became involved in iron mining and other mercantile ventures. Courtesy of the Clinton County Historical Museum

Capt. William Wallace Wood led his company in the Civil War battles of Bull Run and Chancellorsville. After being mustered out in 1863 he returned to Woods Falls where he began construction of an iron forge with his partners Amasa Wood and Frank Palmer. He was a prosperous businessman in Clinton County for many years. Courtesy of Special Collections, Feinberg Library, SUNY, Plattsburgh

increasing tensions. A North-South split in the Methodist, Presbyterian, and Baptist denominations occurred. The Underground Railroad still operated across the county to Canada. State politics were increasingly splintered by the slavery issue, and in 1855 a new anti-slavery party, the Republican, appeared on the ballot. The presidential election of 1860 brought the political divisions to a head, and Clinton County supported Abraham Lincoln.

Three days after the Fort Sumter action on April 12, 1861, Lincoln issued his first call for volunteers couched, as always during his first year, in terms of preserving the Union. By April 26 the first company left Plattsburgh for Albany, public subscriptions paying their expenses. Within a few days another company was raised in Plattsburgh, and a third in Mooers. All of them elected their own officers before they departed. In Albany the three companies were merged with others from Franklin and St. Lawrence counties to create the Sixteenth Regiment, the first to be formed in northern New York.

After receiving several weeks of rigorous training, the regiment reached Washington at the end of June, just in time for the first battle of Bull Run. As a part of the Army of the Potomac, the regiment was involved, sometimes with heavy losses, in the prolonged and discouraging Peninsular campaign, and at Antietam, Fredericksburg and Chancellorsville before its two-year enlistments expired. During its last five months its chaplain was the Rev. Frank Hall, who had married the Delord granddaughter and who later settled in Plattsburgh to minister to a splinter group from the Presbyterian church. The regiment sustained losses of more than 10 percent killed or mortally wounded and 24 percent wounded but recovered. The many letters back to families and friends complained of homesickness, the boredom of camp life interrupted by the horrors of battle and, always, the pervasive illnesses from inadequate food, shelter, and sanitary facilities.

During the first winter of the war the Ninety-sixth Regiment was organized at the Plattsburgh Barracks. Forres Fisher, in a letter to his cousin Cornelius in East Beekmantown, explained that he volunteered to head off a draft which might be needed because so many of his neighbors had fled to Canada to avoid military service.

The regiment was in Virginia in time for the Peninsular campaign in the spring, followed by campaigns in North Carolina. At the end of their two-year enlistments, the men reenlisted, but only after first receiving veterans' furloughs to Plattsburgh. Three months after their return to duty in the spring of 1864, the toll of sharpshooters and the hot, dry weather had reduced the numbers fit for duty to 145. The unit took part in the prolonged seige of Petersburg and the capture of Richmond. After the war the men completed their enlistment time by guard duty in the South.

Stephen Moffitt, a native of Clintonville, was the first man to enlist in the Ninety-sixth. He entered the army as a private and left it as a colonel, with a brevet commission to Brigadier General. As a lieutenant colonel he lost a leg at Fair Oaks while carrying a disabled private from the field. For some months he was a prisoner of war at Libby prison and elsewhere in the South. After the war he became a distinguished citizen of Plattsburgh.

War came directly to the North Country in a curious fashion. In October 1864 a band of Confederate soldiers operating from Canada raided St. Albans, Vermont and got away with large sums of money from the town's three banks. It was later learned that the raid had once been planned for Plattsburgh but was called off when someone remembered that there was a military installation there. The raid caused panic in the border towns, and in Plattsburgh a Home Guard was mobilized which patrolled the streets for the rest of the winter. Its only casualty came when one of the men on duty shot himself in the foot.

These were the color bearers of the Sixteenth New York Volunteers who fought in the Civil War. The flags were made by Plattsburgh ladies. Courtesy of Plattsburgh Public Library

Behind a company of soldiers drawn up at the Plattsburgh Barracks is the Stone Barracks, now listed in the National Register of Historic Places. The structure on the left was subsequently demolished. Courtesy of the Clinton County Historical Museum

Long abandoned and desolate, this one-room schoolhouse is located on the Rock Road in Plattsburgh. Courtesy of the Clinton County Historical Museum

Pupils and their principal, Mr. Miller, posed for a formal group photograph at the Oak Street School in Plattsburgh. Courtesy of the Clinton County Historical Museum

Adirondack Mills, at Lapham Mills, was a prosperous concern in the nineteenth century. Courtesy of Special Collections, Feinberg Library, SUNY Plattsburgh

The Queen of the Harvest Company manufactured agricultural implements at West Chazy. In this photograph three seed cleaning and winnowing machines sit on a wagon ready for distribution. Courtesy of the Clinton County Historical Museum

Workers stand outside the Peru gristmill, one of many such mills in the county. Courtesy of Peru Free Library

A view of the charcoal kilns at the Narrows of Chateaugay Lake includes children on the dock in foreground. Special Collections, Feinberg Library, SUNY Plattsburgh

An early blast furnace west of Peru was operated by the Ketchum family before passing into the hands of the Signors. Courtesy of Special Collections, Feinberg Library, SUNY, Plattsburgh

The iron works at Arnold Hill was extremely important in the area's early economy. It provided jobs and stability until Arnold Hill became a ghost town in the late 1800s. Courtesy of Special Collections, Feinberg Library, SUNY, Plattsburgh

An oil painting of the arch bridge in Keeseville by Charles C. Ellenwood also depicts the river's tumbling waters and the Au Sable Horse Nail headquarters, which was crowned by an eagle (at the top right). Courtesy of Mr. & Mrs. George Brewer

Duane Hamilton Hurd illustrated the Saranac Horse Nail Company's factory in his book History of Clinton and Franklin Counties, 1880. *Iron mining and the manufacture of iron products was a principal industry in Clinton County at that time.*

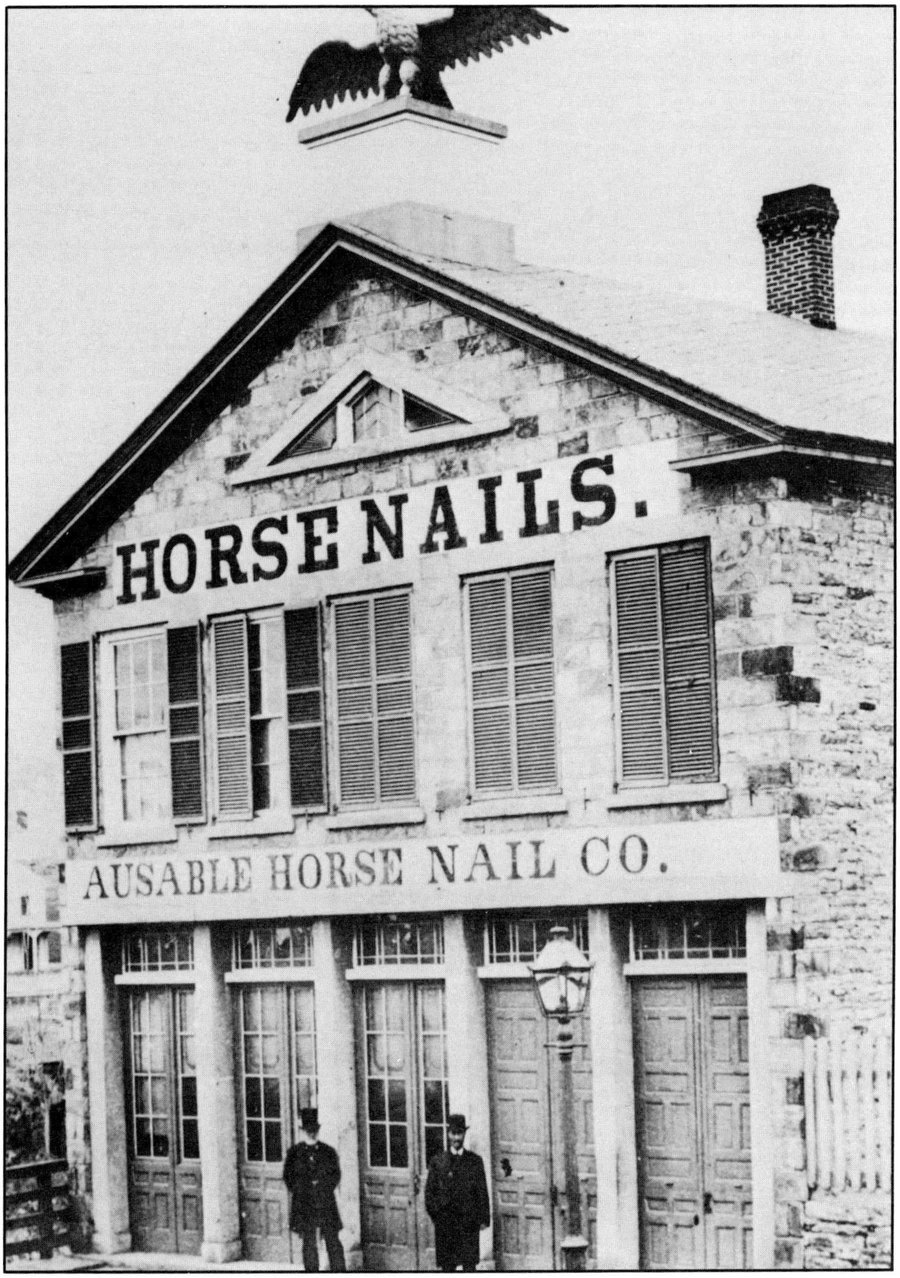

The AuSable Horse Nail Company's building still exists in Keeseville, but no one seems to know what happened to the splendid eagle on top. Courtesy of Special Collections, Feinberg Library, SUNY, Plattsburgh

Plattsburgh, N. Y., Oct 1 1872

Bought of SOWLES & EDWARDS,

Dealers in Heavy and Shelf

Hardware, Iron, Steel, Nails,

Paints, Oils, Glass, Powder, Shot, Lead Pipe, Sheet Lead, Cordage, Oakum, Leather Belting, Lace Leather, &c.

Agents for Sanborn's Steam Safe, Schaghticoke Powder Company and Warren's Roofing.

55 MARGARET STREET.

20# Oakum 12 2 60

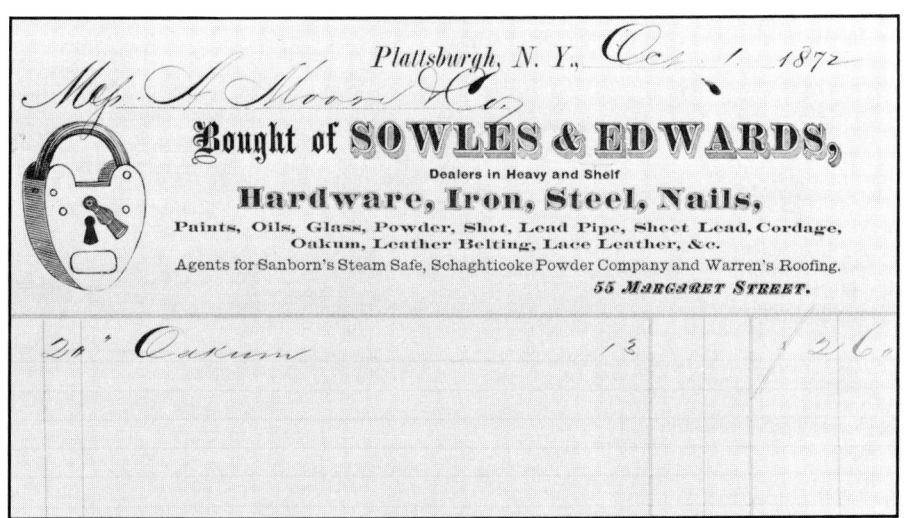

A billhead of 1872 is interesting proof of the importance of hardware stores in the community. Messrs. Sowles and Edwards were prosperous merchants who built stately Victorian residences in Plattsburgh. Courtesy of the Clinton County Historical Museum

A horse ferry, powered by sail, carried passengers and vehicles across the lake in 1870. Courtesy of Richard Ward

Teachers and pupils gathered in front of Morrisonville school for a formal portrait in the late nineteenth century. Note the little girl in the front row with her hands on her hips wearing a wide brimmed hat. Courtesy of the Clinton County Historical Museum

Clinton County Court House, one of three such buildings on the corner of Court and Margaret streets, was destroyed by fire and replaced with the existing Old Court House in 1889. Courtesy of the Clinton County Historical Museum

The Cumberland Hotel, on the corner of Court and Margaret streets in Plattsburgh, was one of the city's grand hotels. It was destroyed by fire and the location is now a parking lot. Courtesy of Special Collections, Feinberg Library, SUNY, Plattsburgh

Section IV Peace and Prosperity

The Adirondack *was one of several sidewheel steamboats plying the waters of Lake Champlain in the nineteenth century. Courtesy of Special Collections, Feinberg Library, SUNY, Plattsburgh*

1870-1880

Eighteen-seventy brought a measure of tranquility to Clinton County. The war was over, and agriculture was still a major way of earning a living. But change was coming to the area—changes that enlarged the scope and in some ways, particularly in Lyon Mountain and Standish, changed the face of Clinton County.

Industry and its solid accompaniment—new capital—was increasing in the county. And linking this to the outside world came the Western Union Telegraph Company, setting up a Plattsburgh office in 1871.

Transportation played an enormous role in further opening up Clinton County to the rest of the state and to eastern markets. In 1870 the Delaware and Hudson Company leased the steamboats *Rensselaer* and *Saratoga*. In 1867 the company had bought the *Adirondack* and in 1872 the *Vermont II*. There was a very real struggle going on at this time between the Vermont Steamboat Boat Lines, its Boston capitalists, and the railroads. The former two were desperately militating against the building of a railroad line coming from the south and linking with Plattsburgh and Rouses Point. However, those backing the railroad won, and a triumphant group of prominent businessmen were the first passengers on November 29, 1875, as the train pulled into Plattsburgh from the south. A huge banquet was held that evening at the splendid Fouquet House with its elegant ballroom and well-appointed rooms. The Honorable Smith M. Weed presided at this celebration dinner. Prominent guests at that banquet included John Jacob Astor, J. Pierpont Morgan, and Cornelius Vanderbilt. The next morning at 8:30, they all boarded the train and traveled north to Rouses Point where a large crowd awaited them. A grand salute suitably crowned the occasion. The train was pulled by the I. V. Baker engine, D&H 4-4-0, No. 126, a locomotive built in Schenectady in 1867, which served as the commemorative special that pulled the first train to northern New York.

Transportation on the lake was also changing. The *Vermont II* set standards in opulence and comfort and was one of the finest steam vessels in its class. But now that trains were serving the northernmost section of the state, boat service through the Narrows near Whitehall and Ticonderoga became redundant. The train era ended the boat monopoly of north-south travel and forced the end of the night lines on steamships.

In 1874, the Transportation Company acquired from the railroads the *Oakes Ames*, a large ferry with two engines and two sets of tracks on the main decks. For six years it carried thousands of railroad cars from Burlington to Plattsburgh by means of an ingenious device called a self-adjusting railroad bridge. This, with the help of a steam engine on shore, could speedily transfer freight cars to the boat. The *Ames* made four daily trips in each direction, saving eighteen miles over the shortest rail route between Boston and Montreal and nearly thirty

Shown here is the interior of the Adirondack's *State Room Hall, resplendent with corinthian columns, mahogany paneling and chandeliers. Courtesy of Special Collections, Feinberg Library, SUNY, Plattsburgh*

The Maquam *was built in 1881 by the St. Johnsbury and Lake Champlain Railroad. It operated between Swanton and Rouses Point as an excursion boat. It was purchased by the Champlain Transportation Company in 1897 to operate between Burlington and St. Albans. In 1897 President William McKinley traveled on the* Maquam *from Hotel Champlain to Isle La Motte. The* Maquam *was retired from service in 1906.*

The other ship is the Vermont II *built in 1871 at Shelburne Harbor for the Lake Champlain Transportation Company. Retired in 1903, it was called the most satisfactory steamer operated by the company on the lake. Courtesy of Special Collections, Feinberg Library, SUNY, Plattsburgh*

between Boston and Ogdensburg. When the railroad line to Plattsburgh and Rouses Point was completed, the railroads no longer needed the big sidewheeler.

Ships still plied their traffic, both human and freight, over Lake Champlain. Many stories are still told about the sudden massive waves that sprang up on it and threatened shipping, as well as stories that reflect the heroism of the lake captains and their crews.

Opening the county through railroads and telegraphs also heralded the advent of new industry. The Chateaugay Ore Company opened its doors in 1873. (It was later renamed the Chateaugay Ore and Iron Company.) When taken over by the company's officers, it opened up a plank road seventy-three miles long into almost impenetrable forest land and set up a huge steam Catalan forge of eighteen fires at Belmont. The villages of Lyon Mountain and Standish came into being. The company owned 33,000 acres of this wilderness, and later owned 30,000 more acres of land. This included a great vein of iron 2,600 feet in length with a working surface of 40,000 feet from which 800 tons were raised daily. There were charcoal blast furnaces there and in Plattsburgh. There was work for three hundred men in Standish while three hundred to four hundred more men worked in the forest cutting up pulp wood. The railroad was extended from Plattsburgh to Dannemora, supplanting the plank road. Lyon Mountain grew to a thriving village of three-thousand people—the busiest spot in Clinton County. Officers of the Chateaugay Ore and Iron Company were Smith M. Weed, Talbot Olyphant, and Frank F. Smith. The general manager was James N. Stower. As company towns owning both houses and the company store, Lyon Mountain and Standish were busy places indeed.

But Lyon Mountain was not the only place in Clinton County experiencing a boom. Amasa and Wallace Wood and Frank Palmer opened an iron forge at Wood's Falls. Sixteen charcoal kilns provided fuel for the fires and water power was diverted from the river. The Woods bought out Frank Palmer, and in 1874 there was a forge, two sawmills, a starch mill, lathe and shingle mill, with preparations being made for a charcoal-producing plant. Again the company built its own houses and stores. Forty teams of horses were kept in what was described as the "largest barn in the Town of Mooers." It was said that when the Woods Falls forge was in use, residents didn't have to use their lamps at night as the large fires from the forge gave ample light.

Arnold Hill had a population of five hundred people, predominately Welsh. The Arnold Hill Ore Bed was under operation, and in Au Sable Forks the J and J Rogers Iron Ore Company was in business and had also established a company town. The huge Catalan forges illuminated the area.

There were three starch factories in Chazy. Starch was made from potatoes brought in by farmers who sold them for twenty cents a bushel until scarcity sent the price up to twenty-five cents. It is reported that every road leading to the factories was filled with wagons loaded with potatoes. The starch was sold to cotton mills in Massachusetts and Rhode Island.

Lumber mills and retail stores also made an impact on the county. In 1876 E. S. Arnold purchased a large building in Peru in which he sold parlor stoves and cookstoves. At that time the largest cash crop in Peru was potatoes, raised for starch. Baker Brothers, lumber dealers, began a retail trade in timber and lumber in Plattsburgh about this time.

The nucleus of a medical community in the county was becoming more evident with Dr. David Kellogg and Dr. Joseph H. LaRocque coming to Plattsburgh, along with Dr. Arthur, who located his practice in Lyon Mountain.

The legal profession was also augmented with M. H. O'Brien joining the firm of Palmer, Weed, Gay and Holcombe. Thomas F. Conway, later to be a lieutenant-governor of New York State, was also practicing law at that time.

In the 1870s it was still a rural community with social life fashioned around the sleighing, bob-sledding, and skating in the winter, singing and simple parties juxtaposed with elegant evening soirees for the wealthy, county fairs, and strawberry socials in summer. But most importantly it was a time of preparation, of excitement, of company organizations, of men with vision who sought wealth and opportunity for the decades of luxury ahead.

Nineteenth-century travel by boat on Lake Champlain was extensive—by oar, by sail, by steam. In an old print of the waterfront at Rouses Point, the Station House Hotel awaits passengers disembarking from a variety of vessels. Courtesy of the Clinton County Historical Museum

Amasa B. Wood, brother of William Wallace Wood, became sufficiently prosperous to build himself an elegant mansion in West Chazy. From History of Clinton and Franklin Counties, *1880, D. H. Hurd.*

The Davern House in Peru was a well-known hotel for travelers on these unimproved roads in 1875. Courtesy of the Peru Free Library

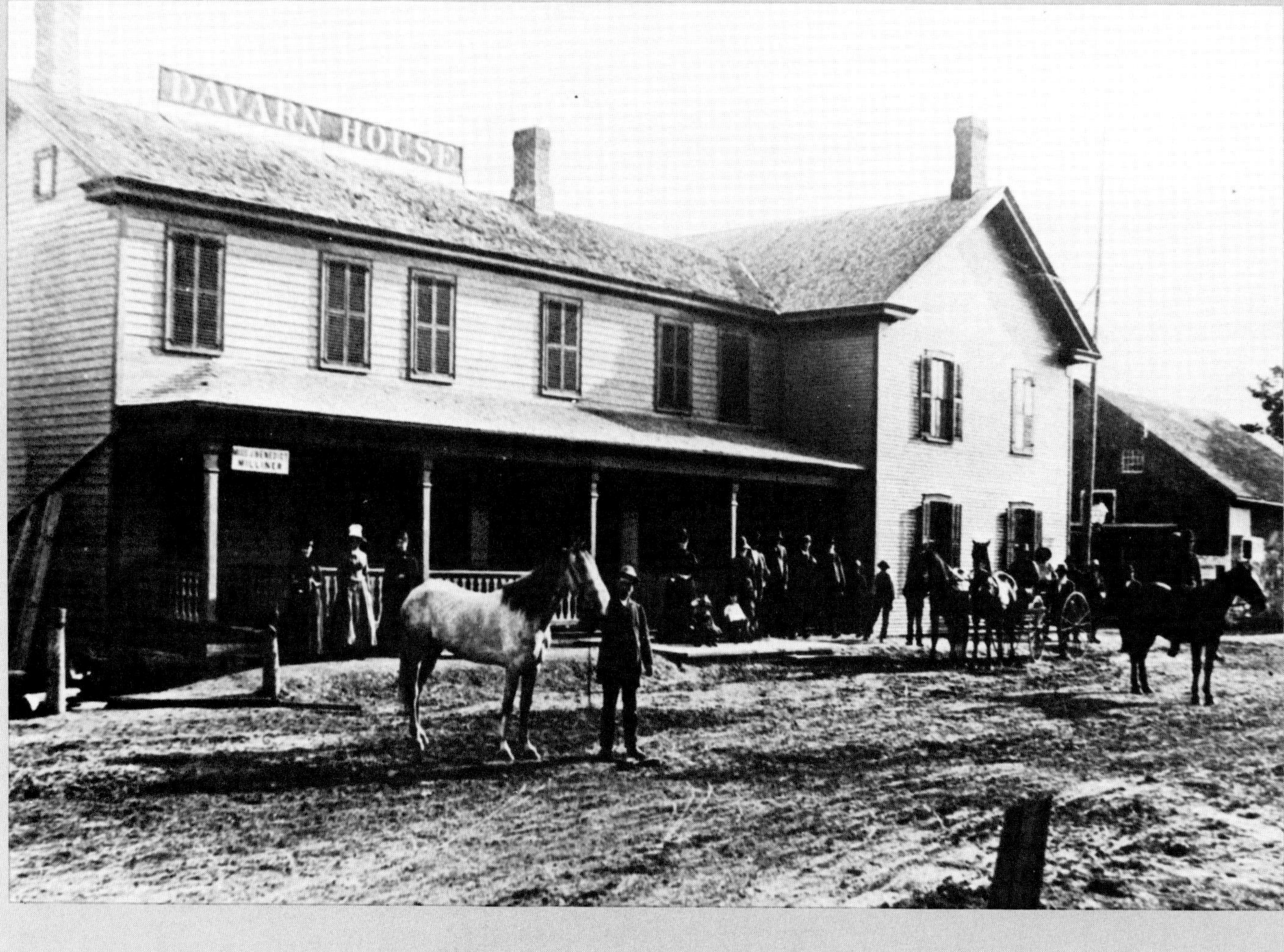

Plattsburgh Academy and High School are shown here circa 1875. An older academy which stood on this spot was a two-story frame building, built in 1811. The new academy served until 1914, at which time a new high school was opened on Broad Street, at the south end of Oak Street. Courtesy of the Clinton County Historical Museum

This "bird's-eye" view of Plattsburgh in 1877 was drawn by A. Ruger. The lithograph was made by the C. H. Vogt Company of Milwaukee and was published by J. J. Stoner, Madison, Wisconsin. Most of the village is still confined to the area bounded by Broad, Beekman and Cornelia streets and the river. Note the two islands located in the river where the sewage treatment plant now stands. Courtesy of the Clinton County Historical Museum

J. W. Tuttle, a Plattsburgh printer, produced many elegant announcements of social events, such as this invitation to the Independence Ball at West Chazy in 1872. Addressed to gentlemen, it encouraged them to bring a partner. Courtesy of the Clinton County Historical Museum

A stereograph view of the Champlain II *after it was shipwrecked at Steam Mill Point in 1875. Although the pilot, John Eldridge, was a skilled navigator, evidence at the inquiry revealed that he may have been addicted to morphine. It was generally believed that Eldridge had been in a drugged state at the time of the wreck, and his license was revoked. Courtesy of Special Collections, Feinberg Library, SUNY, Plattsburgh*

The Parsons and Cheney Store, next to Scofield's Grocery, in 1874 was a Saranac shop; Fred Parsons was the original proprietor. Courtesy of the Clinton County Historical Museum

A supper menu from the American House laid heavy emphasis on hearty meals for travelers. It had thirty-one bedrooms and a dining room that seated fifty. There were electric lights and steam heat throughout, and a stable that accommodated one hundred horses. Rates were two dollars a day. The hotel, at No. 16 and 18 River Street, was near the railroad station and handy for commercial travelers in Plattsburgh. Courtesy of the Clinton County Historical Museum

The trolley waits and horse-drawn carriages are drawn up at the Delaware and Hudson Railroad Depot, awaiting the arrival of passengers. They would then be conveyed to any one of the several hotels in town. Courtesy of Mary G. Leggett

An illustration from Duane H. Hurd's History of Clinton and Franklin Counties, *1880, depicts Cold Spring Farm at Champlain, owned by Lemuel North.*

The tannery at Altona began its operation around 1860. Started by Stephen and Frank Dow, it was then bought by Clark and Company of Chateaugay and sold again to D. M. Dizer and Company of Boston, Massachusetts. Joseph Pyper was the manager. The tannery was on the east bank of the Chazy River, and a large dam supplied water for the operation. It was a prosperous business; in fact, the only drawback was the smell. It closed about 1900. Courtesy of Special collections, Feinberg Library, SUNY Plattsburgh

The reason for this outdoor female gathering is not known, but it appears to be a pleasant occasion. Courtesy of the Peru Free Library

Elmer F. Elmore grew up to become a prominent Peru businessman. In this studio portrait he is dressed as Little Lord Fauntleroy. Courtesy of the Clinton County Historical Museum

The Schuyler Falls Band turned out in their finest, topped with derby hats, ready to assume their position in the local parade in 1880. Courtesy of the Clinton County Historical Museum

Advertising was blunt and to the point in the 1870s. The sign above the doorway of this store in Mooers warns the customer that credit is not available. Courtesy of Special Collections, Feinberg Library, SUNY, Plattsburgh

Courtesy of the Clinton County Historical Museum

Winslow photo courtesy of Special Collections, Feinberg Library, SUNY Plattsburgh

Known as the Turner House, this building was constructed by Ebenezer S. Winslow on Cornelia Street, Plattsburgh. Construction took place in 1876-77 and contains the black walnut fireplace which Winslow saw at the centennial exhibition in Philadelphia in 1876, and ordered for delivery after the fair closed. The architecture of the house is High Gothic, that of the carriage house in the background is Italianate. The house has been demolished but the carriage house is still standing. Courtesy of the Clinton County Historical Museum

The Clinton County Agricultural Society annually announced a number of awards for exhibits at the county fair. This 1888 diploma honors the Smith brothers for their fur exhibit. The society and its annual fairs were introduced in 1819. Courtesy of the Clinton County Fair

Chapter 5

1880-1890

The 1880s opened with a bang. In 1886 an explosion at the Clinton County Powder Works, located at the Maine Mill, rocked the center of Plattsburgh and hurled large stones into the air. The dynamite factory was demolished and rebuilt—but exploded again in 1887, whereupon it was moved from Clinton County. Fortunately, no one was killed in either explosion.

The Clinton County Fairgrounds were established in Plattsburgh in 1886 on what was known as Boynton's farm at the north end of Oak Street. The yearly fairs brought in people from all over the county to vie for prizes for vegetables and fruit, homemade cakes and pies, jellies, jams, pickles, etc. There was also horseracing for the gentlemen to enjoy, and many placed wagers upon their favorite horses.

The Northern New York Telephone Company opened its doors in 1880 and this, together with the telegraph, opened more communication with the rest of the state and Vermont.

The cheese factory in Peru, operated by the A.D. Boomhower Creamery, was in full operation and provided more employment to the people living there.

In Plattsburgh many retail establishments had been added. Cady's and O.T. Larkin's drug stores and the Medical Hall, belonging to Dr. Gilbert, boasted elaborate soda fountains where the youth (and not so young) of the area gathered. Dry goods stores and millinery stores sprang up on Margaret Street. By 1889 Plattsburgh Light, Heat and Power Company supplied electric light for streets, houses, businesses and industries. The Plattsburgh Philharmonic Society, conducted by Charles F. Hudson, came into being in 1883, as did many cultural societies and fraternal organizations.

Blacksmiths were in urgent demand all through the county to shoe the hundreds of horses bringing iron ore from remote mines and forges to Plattsburgh for local manufacturers or to the lake barges to be shipped farther away.

In 1888 the Williams Sewing Machine Company, which had begun as a joint stock part of a Canadian firm, and had earlier made 25 to 50 machines a week, made 350 to 400 machines weekly and hired about eight hundred people. Later this company made typewriters in its factory on the banks of the Saranac in Plattsburgh.

In Beekmantown, Chazy, Mooers, Champlain, Rouses Point—indeed wherever the railroad touched—there were cattle yards where the farmers could keep the cattle destined for market. Huge hay barns were built near the yards to store feed. In Beekmantown the Conroys, Reynolds, and other well-known farmers erected their own buildings.

Small one-room schoolhouses with their adjacent privies dotted the landscape. High school students could

An advertisement announces a performance on Friday, May 16, 1883, of "The Messiah," fifth concert. The organization had not performed prior to that year. Courtesy of Special Collections, Feinberg Library, SUNY, Plattsburgh

take the daily train to Plattsburgh, paying a fifteen-cent fare from Beekmantown to Plattsburgh.

General stores were in every village now, carrying groceries, dry goods, clothing, thread, farm machinery, fertilizer and, of course, penny candy. Many farmers had sugar maples on their land. Maple syrup and sugar were produced to trade at the stores for goods or sold directly from wagons. Men traded cord wood and fence posts for merchandise at the general store while women traded eggs and butter.

Fires were a constant threat. In 1877 a fire in Cannon Corners burnt houses, barns, sawmills, a wood yard, a church, and the bridge. Had it not been finally checked by the wind, which had shifted, it would have consumed both Mooers Forks and Mooers.

Wood's Falls with its huge forge began to dwindle in importance as the lumber supply was depleted and other sources of iron became more available elsewhere at cheaper rates. Eventually, it had only one house remaining to signify that once it was a busy, bustling place.

Professions were well represented by now in Clinton County. Churches of all denominations were built in the county, and all the clergy became an even more important element in the community. More physicians had settled here and formed an association. Lawyers also settled here in active practice, using Plattsburgh, the county seat—with its county courthouse and the adjacent buildings for the county clerk and the surrogate judge—as a center for business.

The Plattsburgh Traction Company began operating a trolley system on July 4, 1896 in Plattsburgh; the Delaware and Hudson Railroad took over the entire system by 1906. With six and one-half miles of single track, ten passenger cars, four box vestibule cars, the trolley industry became an important part of public travel in the city. Every fifteen minutes from 8 a.m. to 11 p.m., a

This is St. Mary's Catholic Church, Champlain, as it appeared in 1880. Courtesy of Special Collections, Feinberg Library, SUNY, Plattsburgh

trolley car would leave the station, pick up passengers and drop them off at various points in the city. A nickel's ride would take you from Delaware and Hudson Railroad (the depot was built in 1886 at a cost of $22,000) up Bridge Street to Margaret Street, then Broad Street past St. John's Church and the Home for the Friendless to Beekman Street and the Normal School, down Cornelia Street to Platt Street (Montcalm) to the Fairgrounds on Bailey Avenue and completing the loop back to Bridge Street. Summer hours became effective when resorts opened. On a summer's eve you could, for a dime, hop the Buffalo car at Cady's Corners and take the trip to Clinton Park, home of the local baseball team, and watch the local lads take on the Malone team or any of the other teams that made up the Northern New York League. The Plattsburgh Traction Company put on extra cars for these events and sold coupon tickets good for transportation and admission to the event. If your destination was the Catholic Summer School, that was the next stop when you disembarked to a canopied platform to attend a lecture or performance, then on to Hotel Champlain for a hop or a party in the opulent ballroom.

In 1906 the Plattsburgh Traction Company became the property of the Delaware and Hudson Railroad Company through stock purchases. The succeeding years saw much growth in the trolley system, with new cars being added to the line and track improvements until 1920 when the system became unprofitable. The Delaware and Hudson threatened to abandon the trolley system in 1925, forcing Plattsburgh businesses to consider purchasing the company. At that time, in an effort to save the failing company, the Honorable J. F. O'Brien and Corydon Johnson purchased it and made changes, but to no avail. On Monday, November 11, 1929, the last trolley car left its berth for a final ride. The advent of the automobile had made the trolley obsolete.

The New York State Legislature passed a bill in 1889 establishing a State Normal School in Plattsburgh. The Legislature authorized sixty thousand dollars for the school and the county supervisors gave three thousand dollars for the land. Construction started immediately on a building located on Beekman Street in Plattsburgh. It was a three-story structure with classrooms for students in the Model school on the first floor; classrooms for Normal School students, lecture halls, laboratories and auditoriums were on the second and third floors. Tuition and textbooks were free. The first principal was Professor Fox Holden.

In 1929 fire destroyed the building, and the present Hawkins Hall opened in 1932. The course had now been lengthened from two years to three years. In 1938 the Normal School became a four-year degree-granting teachers' college. In 1948 State University of New York was established, and the Plattsburgh college became a unit in the system.

All aboard to the Barracks, Clinton Park, Bluff Point, and Fairgrounds, at five cents to ten cents a ride. Courtesy of the Clinton County Historical Museum

The Fouquet House stood in close proximity to the Delaware and Hudson Railroad Station on Bridge Street, Plattsburgh. Courtesy of the Clinton County Historical Museum

A portrait of Professor George H. Hudson, head of the Department of Science at the old Normal School, shows him as an elderly gentleman. Dr. Hudson's family was well-known in the area for its musical talent. Courtesy of Special Collections, Feinberg Library, SUNY, Plattsburgh

A charming picture of three generations was taken from a tintype. The unidentified family lived in Cooperville and the men seem to have been of sporting persuasion. Courtesy of Craig Koste

Shown here are Plattsburgh livery stables from which Dr. Kellogg, in his later years, sometimes hired a driver and wagon for his night calls into the country. Special Collections, Feinberg Library, SUNY Plattsburgh

Keeseville Village is shown here before the fire of 1882. On the left is the Congregational Church and Hewitt's Hotel. Courtesy of Special Collections, Feinberg Library, SUNY, Plattsburgh

Workers congregate for a group photograph in front of the Isham Carriage Works in 1881. The Isham cushioned wagon spring was manufactured for the lumber wagons, buggies and cutters that were produced here in 1890. Courtesy of the Clinton County Historical Museum

Dr. David S. Kellogg wrote in his journal of late nineteenth-century excursions to scenic areas such as the top of Lyon Mountain (3,830 feet). Courtesy of Special Collections, Feinberg Library, SUNY, Plattsburgh

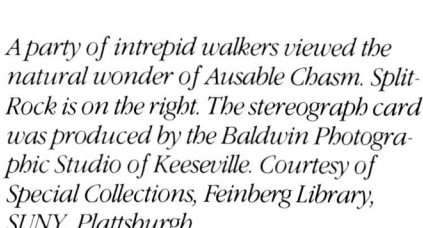

A party of intrepid walkers viewed the natural wonder of Ausable Chasm. Split-Rock is on the right. The stereograph card was produced by the Baldwin Photographic Studio of Keeseville. Courtesy of Special Collections, Feinberg Library, SUNY, Plattsburgh

The Kennedy house in Altona was photographed in the late 1880s. The photograph shows Mr. Eugene Kennedy, an employee of the Delaware and Hudson Railroad, with his daughter. Courtesy of Special Collections, Feinberg Library, SUNY, Plattsburgh

George Meserve, above, was too young to enlist in the Civil War but he went to the battlefield to take care of horses and deliver mail until he was old enough to be a soldier. He later drove a coach for President Garfield. He drove for Paul Smith's from 1880 to 1890, and was called "the famous whip of the Adirondacks." His first home was in Plattsburgh, then he and his family moved to Keeseville where he is buried. Courtesy of the Clinton County Historical Museum

The original Customs House and Post Office, located at the corner of Brinkerhoff and Margaret streets, was replaced by the Plattsburgh Federal Building. Courtesy of the Clinton County Historical Museum

W. W. Hartwell was a prominent Clinton County businessman who owned a splendid mansion on Brinkerhoff Street in Plattsburgh, now the Regina Maria Retreat House. Mr. and Mrs. Hartwell and their friends were intrepid nineteenth-century travelers who enjoyed viewing scenery at first hand. Courtesy of Special Collections, Feinberg Library, SUNY, Plattsburgh

The girded framework supporting the tracks used by the cars delivering ore from the mines in Lyon Mountain provides a skeletal background in this early picture of the Chateaugay Ore and Iron

These miners are being taken down the shaft on a double deck man skip. This picture was taken at the Chateaugay Ore and Iron company mines in Lyon Mountain. Courtesy of the Clinton County Historical Museum

An unusual celebration took place at the mines by torchlight, with a full orchestra and costumed choral group. The reason is unknown. Courtesy of Special Collections, Feinberg Library, SUNY, Plattsburgh

Company, later to become Republic Steel. In 1899 the president of the Chateaugay Ore and Iron Company was Smith M. Weed. Courtesy of the Clinton County Historical Museum

The Singing Sands Beach was a major attraction for guests at Hotel Champlain in 1900. Courtesy of the Clinton County Historical Museum

1890-1900

If each decade wrought more changes in Clinton County, none did more so than the last ten years of the nineteenth century. And it had its quota of famous visitors to the area, now becoming known for its clean air, beautiful lake, and woodland areas.

In 1892 President Benjamin Harrison and his wife were on their way to Loon Lake for a summer stay. President Harrison spoke to an enthusiastic crowd assembled at the Fouquet House in Plattsburgh. William Dean Howells, the noted author, was a visitor in the area also.

A concern for learning and sharing literary knowledge emerged at this time. Reading clubs abounded and members worked assiduously producing papers to be read aloud. A public library was established in 1894 by the Rev. N. Richards who opened a reading room in the Baptist Church's basement. Books were augmented by the state's traveling library. Soon it had village support and grew to fifteen hundred volumes by 1898 and had moved to quarters in the Plattsburgh Theatre.

Work began in 1888 on Hotel Champlain, a magnificent edifice located at Bluff Point, a site that rose from a superb woodland of evergreens and was elevated a few hundred feet above the lake. A sweeping view of Lake Champlain was afforded from the large verandas of the hotel. The building itself was surrounded by 450 acres of woodland and meadows where roads, walks leading to small wooded glades, the cliffs and the lake shore with its Singing Sands Beach were carefully planned. Seats were placed in suitable nooks so that guests could rest while enjoying the view.

The hotel opened in 1890. It had five hundred rooms, each with a view. All the latest conveniences were provided for guests who usually came and stayed for the summer. It boasted golf courses, tennis courts, and facilities for boating, billiards, bowling, and archery. Many lake steamers stopped at Hotel Champlain to take guests on excursions to Burlington, Ticonderoga, or out among the lake islands.

The hotel was built by the Delaware and Hudson Railroad Corporation and attracted the rich and famous to its doors. In 1897 President McKinley and his wife, Vice-President Hobart and his wife, and Secretary of War Alger made Hotel Champlain the summer White House. They did so for two summers.

Another hotel that figures prominently at that time was the Witherill Hotel in Plattsburgh, run by William T. Howell and kept in business for years by the Howell family. Spacious and elegant, it was known for its comfortable rooms and excellent dining. The American House on River Street in the city was also popular and was situated conveniently near the railroad depot, as was the Cumberland House. By now there were hotels in every village or hamlet in the county, with some boarding houses available as well.

Hotel Champlain, frequented by presidents and many illustrious Americans, was one of the great hotels in and around the Adirondacks which was built in the late nineteenth century to accommodate summer vacationers. Harper's Weekly chose to feature it on the magazine's front cover. Courtesy of the Clinton County Historical Museum

Vice-President Garrett Hobart's wife serves tea to guests during her stay at Hotel Champlain in the summer of 1897. Courtesy of the Clinton County Historical Museum

At Cliff Haven, a few miles south of Plattsburgh, on 450 acres of lakeside property, with wooded bluffs, sand beach, a bay suitable for anchoring all kinds of lake-going vessels as well as the popular canoes and rowboats, stood the Catholic Summer School of America. It was the culmination of an idea born in Catholic reading circles and the Catholic Chautauqua movement, and it resulted in establishing a summer school whose purpose was to expand the work for higher education. The school received its charter from the Regents of the State of New York on February 9, 1893.

The Catholic Summer School's first sessions were held in the Plattsburgh Theatre. Attendance increased every year and by 1896 an auditorium and several cottages had been built at Cliff Haven and the sessions moved there. More cottages were built as well as a chapel, a clubhouse, a casino, boarding houses, tennis courts, and a nine-hole golf course. Cottages ranged from the simple to the very elegant. At the Champlain Club and its annex in 1910, rooms were one dollar a week and up. Meals cost eleven dollars a week. An orchestra played during dinner on Sundays and three other evenings each week, while formal dances were held every Wednesday evening.

The main emphasis was on education with courses in astronomy, art, music, philosophy, literature, French, and physical culture. However, swimming, tennis, golf, cycling, mountain climbing, and boating were very much included in the residents' lives. The steamer *Ticonderoga* took visitors on lake excursions in 1910 for fifty cents per passenger. Expeditions were also planned to places as far away as Quebec City and the Shrine of St. Anne de Beaupre. Accommodations for fifteen hundred people were provided.

President McKinley and Vice-President Hobart are seated in a carriage on the dock at Hotel Champlain during the summer of 1897. Courtesy of the Clinton County Historical Museum

Local dignitaries greeted President William McKinley and Vice-President Garrett Hobart at the Hotel Champlain Station in 1897. From the rear on the car platform are: Smith M. Weed, Mrs. Hobart (with bouquet), Mrs. McKinley (partially hidden), unidentified woman (in doorway), President McKinley, and Vice-President Hobart (on bottom step). From the left on the ground are: Railroad Conductor Long, J. N. Stower (partially hidden), unidentified boy (with cap), Inman Stower (with hat), Mr. Seaver (manager of Hotel Champlain), George Weed, unidentified man, unidentified child, and unidentified man. Courtesy of the Clinton County Historical Museum

91

The Witherill Hotel on Margaret Street, Plattsburgh, opened in 1886. It offered some of the finest accommodations for travelers in Clinton County. Courtesy of the Clinton County Historical Museum

Built in the 1890s, the Hotel Windsor (later the Saxony) in Rouses Point was an elegant summer resort in its prime. Helen Mayo Mero, who celebrates her ninety-first birthday in 1988, has childhood recollections of it when her father, Jean Baptiste Mayo, ran the hotel. Courtesy of Special Collections, Feinberg Library, SUNY, Plattsburgh

This picture of the Champlain Club, Catholic Summer School at Cliff Haven, was probably taken an August 15, 1900 for the Feast of the Assumption. Rev. Father Connity, president of the school, is at the right of the altar and Mr. Warren Mosher of Ohio, founder and secretary of the club, is at the left. Courtesy of the Clinton County Historical Museum

Thousands came from the eastern United States and foreign countries. Among prominent visitors were Presidents McKinley and Taft, Governors Theodore Roosevelt and Hughes, and Ambassador J. J. Jusserand from France. The poet Joyce Kilmer visited here and it is said he derived the inspiration for his famous poem "Trees" at Cliff Haven.

The Catholic Summer School grew and prospered until the 1930s when social changes and perhaps the advent of touring by automobile changed the pattern of season-long summer vacations at one resort. Developers purchased the property, after years of disuse, and the cottages, clubs, and auditoriums were demolished in order to create the housing development of Cliff Haven.

On April 5, 1893, the Plattsburgh Theatre on the corner of Marion and Court streets opened its doors to the people of Plattsburgh and Clinton County. The four-story red brick building that had a seating capacity of 1,002 seats, including orchestra, dress circles, two balconies, and gallery, was a gift from the Honorable Smith M. Weed. With its enormous stage, dressing rooms and electric lights, its attracted many well-known theatrical performers and the public was duly impressed by its elegance. The orchestra from the Twenty-first Infantry provided music for the theatre around the turn of the century. Opening night saw trains bringing people in from the outlying areas to see *The Merchant of Venice*. Tickets were auctioned off and ranged from one hundred dollars to two dollars. The house was packed.

The Sousa Band also appeared here. The Plattsburgh Theatre was indicative of its time, and it attracted theatre, operatic and vaudeville performers of the highest quality to its stage. It also showed silent pictures with organ accompaniment. The theatre was a landmark for many years until it was destroyed by fire in 1928.

It would seem, in retrospect, that the 1890s began to popularize Clinton County as a vacation spot where commodious accommodations were offered from Rouses

Located on Pine Street in Plattsburgh, Plattsburgh Shirt Company employed 175 to 200 workers. It opened in 1893 and was the largest of the C. F. Crosby and Company factories. Dresses and shirts were manufactured at a sister factory in Keeseville. Courtesy of Special Collections, Feinberg Library, SUNY, Plattsburgh

Isaac Merkel owned a tobacco, smokers' supplies and fine ales business at 40 Margaret Street in Plattsburgh. Merkel's Department Store is owned and operated by his descendants. Courtesy of the Clinton County Historical Museum

The Home of the Friendless was located on lower Broad Street in 1897. It was here that orphans lived until they reached their eighteenth birthday. Dressed in their black stockings and walking two by two, they were a familiar sight on Plattsburgh streets. Later, the name was changed to the Children's Home. Courtesy of Special Collections, Feinberg Library, SUNY, Plattsburgh

Plattsburgh's fire chief, Michael John West, and his men stand at the ready in 1896. Courtesy of the Clinton County Historical Museum

Ingenuity knows no bounds, as this gentleman demonstrates with his folding fire escape. No evidence exists to suggest his invention was ever patented. Courtesy of Craig Koste

A water fight staged by Plattsburgh firemen delighted the crowd gathered on Margaret Street to watch the exhibition. Courtesy of Special Collections, Feinberg Library, SUNY, Plattsburgh

Point south to Bluff Point—the forerunner of today's thriving tourist business. There was a difference in 1890, however. People stayed for the season. It was an era of elegance, of formal gardens, of ladies and gentlemen "taking the air," of going to the theatre, of concerts and elaborate balls, of teas and lectures, and of sports befitting a more leisurely age.

Business was still growing as well. The Plattsburgh Shirt Company opened its doors in 1893 and the Plattsburgh Foundry and Machine Company came into existence in 1890. The latter was the only such establishment on the west side of Lake Champlain. It produced plows, cultivators, stoves, harrows and did custom jobs. Payette-Mendelsohn Company, I. Scheier, Levy Brothers, and Isaac Merkel were prospering in the cigar and liquor business along with many new retail stores. General stores abounded in the villages and hamlets of the county. Mooers, by now a village, had built a town hall. By 1897 there was a public high school, a grammar school, an intermediate school, and six elementary schools in Plattsburgh Village.

The large number of churches in Plattsburgh included the Methodist Church, the First Presbyterian Church, St. Peter's Church, St. John's Church, Trinity Episcopal Church, the Baptist Church, the Peristrome Presbyterian Church, and the Jewish Synagogue. There was also a YMCA, sponsored by the Railroad Men's Christian Association.

Fireman William Manning holds his shining trumpet proudly for this picture at the turn of the century. Courtesy of the Clinton County Historical Museum

The men of the Lafayette Hose Company assembled at the corner of Brinkerhoff Street and Marion Street in Plattsburgh to have their picture taken with their fire-fighting equipment in 1890. The barrel on the wheeled cart was obviously used to carry water with which to fight the blaze. Courtesy of the Clinton County Historical Museum

Charitable organizations of the time included the Vilas Home for Aged and Infirm Women and the Home of the Friendless for Children.

A fire department was organized in Rouses Point. In 1891 two hose carts were purchased, followed by the purchase of two forty-foot ladders in 1893. The Rouses Point Rescue Hook and Ladder Company and the Montgomery Hose were in operation by 1894.

Fire departments—all volunteer—were organized in other villages at about the same time to protect the citizens. Plattsburgh Village had a fire department as well as a police department. There were fire alarm boxes at the following locations:

- No.   7 - Corner of Brinkerhoff and Catherine streets
- No. 14 - Normal School
- No. 16 - Corner of Brinkerhoff and William streets
- No. 25 - Corner of Lorraine Street and Sailly Avenue
- No. 36 - Baker Brothers' Mill Office
- No. 38 - Sewing Machine Factory
- No. 43 - Corner of Platt and Cornelia streets
- No. 54 - Corner of Clinton Block, Margaret Street
- No. 62 - Corner of Battery and Catherine streets
- No. 73 - Corner of Bridge and Peru streets
- No. 81 - Corner of Margaret and Elm streets
- No. 124 - United States Barracks

Fire Department

N. E. Laravie	Chief Engineer
William S. Manning	First Assistant
Paul Bressette	Second Assistant
John A. McHattie	Secretary
Willis L. Wever	Treasurer
Horicon Engine and Hose Company	60 men
Relief Hose Company	40 men

Smith M. Weed, lawyer and industrialist, had a private park, beautifully landscaped in the formal manner, on the bank of the Saranac River in Plattsburgh in 1895. Courtesy of Special Collections, Feinberg Library, SUNY, Plattsburgh

Lafayette Hose Company . . . . 40 men
Citizen's Hose and H and L
  Company . . . . 100 men
Rescue Hose Company . . . . 40 men

Police Department
M. J. Wool . . . . Chief
Eli Senecal . . . . Patrolman
A. R. Conners . . . . Patrolman
James B. Marsh . . . . Patrolman
William T. Sawyer . . . . Patrolman

A mild season resulting in an ice famine further south led to massive ice-cutting on Lake Champlain during the winter of 1890. The price of ice in the cities skyrocketed and every able-bodied man in Clinton County set out to cut and ship ice on the railroad trains. Ice houses were built up and down the lake to store ice in sawdust. The boom ended when Maine began shipping ice to cities and broke the market.

In 1895 a bicycling craze hit the area and in Plattsburgh indignant citizens demanded laws regulating the speed of bicyclists burning up the roads and endangering pedestrians. As yet there were no public parks in Plattsburgh. There were, however, the parade ground at the Military Post, the grounds at Hotel Champlain, Cliff Haven, and the Normal School. Smith M. Weed had a private park on the river bank in front of his stately home on Cumberland Avenue in Plattsburgh.

The J. and J. Rogers Company of Au Sable Forks had by now incorporated and the company was offering employment to still more men.

Thus the century came to a close amid rejoicing and healthy optimism for the future of Clinton County.

These proud survivors of the Civil War are members of the Walter Benedict Post. Courtesy of the Clinton County Historical Museum

Edward Fisher, his wife Sadie and their daughter, Ethel, stand in front of their home in Beekmantown—a stone house built by Francis Culver in 1814 on Route 22. At the time of the Battle of Plattsburgh in 1814 some wounded British soldiers found shelter in the not-yet-completed house. The Fishers were photographed in 1892. Courtesy of Special Collections, Feinberg Library, SUNY, Plattsburgh

This is the interior of Studholme and Gilmore, Plattsburgh Men's Outfitters which operated from 1892 to 1894. The Studholmes operated men's clothing stores for many years—right up until the 1960s. Here the owners pose casually for the photographer. Courtesy of Special Collections, Feinberg Library, SUNY, Plattsburgh

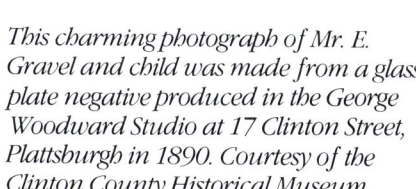

This charming photograph of Mr. E. Gravel and child was made from a glass plate negative produced in the George Woodward Studio at 17 Clinton Street, Plattsburgh in 1890. Courtesy of the Clinton County Historical Museum

This is the Barker homestead in Peru in 1892. Courtesy of Special Collections, Feinberg Library, SUNY, Plattsburgh

Mason's Lumber Yard and Mill occupies a special niche in the history of Peru Village. Courtesy of the Peru Free Library

A hot air balloon ascent was one of the exciting events of the late nineteenth century. Man's efforts to conquer the sky never ceased. Courtesy of Special Collections, Feinberg Library, SUNY, Plattsburgh

A trio of happy fishermen bring home the catch of the day in rural Clinton County. Courtesy of Special Collections, Feinberg Library, SUNY, Plattsburgh

After playing a game of croquet, these officers and their ladies rested long enough to have their pictures taken at the old Plattsburgh Barracks. Courtesy of Special Collections, Feinberg Library, SUNY, Plattsburgh

In the 1890s lumbering was big business in Clinton County. Logs were drawn out of the woods by horsepower, probably destined for the charcoal kilns at Lyon Mountain, Standish or possibly Mooers. Courtesy of Special Collections, Feinberg Library, SUNY, Plattsburgh

The Trombley Brothers operated the largest general store in Altona. Blueberry pickers, in season, brought their berries there to trade for food or other necessities of life. The berries were then shipped by railroad to eastern markets such as Boston. Courtesy of Special Collections Feinberg Library, SUNY, Plattsburgh

These temporary shelters were erected at the blueberry camp in Altona to house the local residents who picked the berries to sell during the season; later these berries were shipped by train to market. Courtesy of Special Collections, Feinberg Library, SUNY, Plattsburgh

The Morning Telegram *office, in 1896, was located at 20 Clinton Street, Plattsburgh. A newspaper was published every day but Sunday. Subscriptions were five dollars per year. Courtesy of the Clinton County Historical Museum*

The bride was beautiful at this wedding breakfast in July 1896. From left to right are George Casper Kellogg, Augusta Kellogg Rogers, William Bowdich Rogers, Effie Tredor, Henry Theodore Kellogg, and Grace Vernon Olyphant Kellogg. Courtesy of Special Collections, Feinberg Library, SUNY, Plattsburgh

A kindergarten class of the Model School was photographed at the Plattsburgh Normal school in 1897. Miss Hamilton was the teacher. Courtesy of Special Collections, Feinberg Library, SUNY, Plattsburgh

Pinafores are worn by both girls and boys in a one-room schoolhouse in 1897. Courtesy of Special Collections, Feinberg Library, SUNY, Plattsburgh

A formal group of officers posed for the camera before leaving for Cuba to fight in the Spanish-American War. Col. George A. Herbst is the first on the left in the fourth row. Note the bearded commanding officer in front row center. Courtesy of Special Collections, Feinberg Library, SUNY, Plattsburgh

This regimental train was leaving for New York City carrying troops trained in Plattsburgh and heading to Cuba in 1898.

The Spanish-American War with the destruction of the battleship Maine led to the slogan "Remember the Maine."

The slogan was then elongated into a children's chant that went as follows:
"Remember the Maine!
To hell with Spain!
And don't forget
To pull the chain!"

The chain to be pulled referred to the overhead water tank of flush toilets during that period. Courtesy of Craig Koste

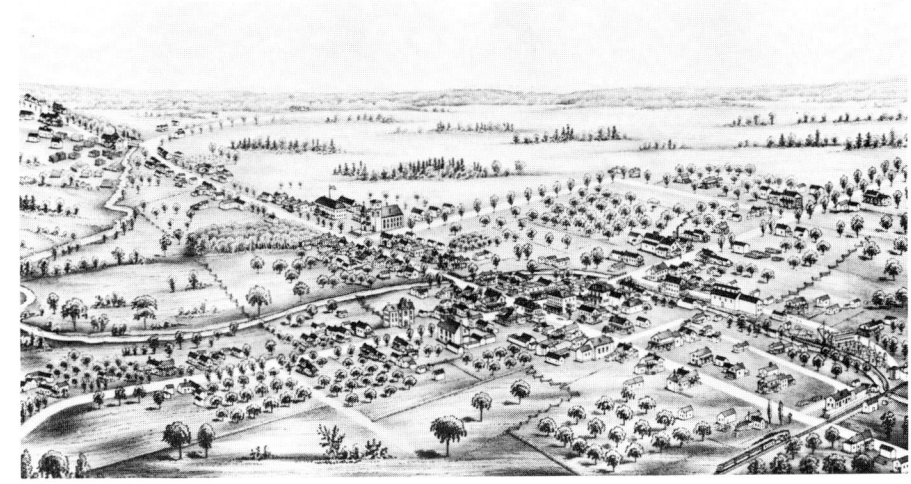

A bird's-eye view of West Chazy is dated 1899. It was drawn and published by G. Fausel of Troy, N.Y.; the lithographer was L. R. Burleigh, also of Troy. Courtesy of the Clinton County Historical Museum

The architecture of the Rouses Point station is typical of the heavy Richardsonian style of the period. This photograph was taken in 1899. Courtesy of the Clinton County Historical Museum

The Western Union Telegraph office was located on Clinton Street at the corner of Marion Street, Plattsburgh, in 1900. Courtesy of the Clinton County Historical Museum

Youngsters gather around the town pump in Peru about 1900. Courtesy of the Peru Free Library

Advertising techniques were used to advantage by the J. Thompson Store in Rouses Point, circa 1900. At the right is a hotel, the Massachusetts House. Courtesy of Julie A. Davies

Young ladies enjoyed boating on Chazy Lake in 1900, while holding umbrellas to protect themselves from the sun. Courtesy of Special Collections, Feinberg Library, SUNY, Plattsburgh

Fort Montgomery, near Rouses Point, is pictured about 1900. The original fort on this site was begun in 1816. However, in 1818 an official survey uncovered the fact that the fort was on Canadian land. Work stopped immediately and it came to be known as Fort Blunder. Under the terms of the 1842 Webster-Ashburton Treaty, the boundary was adjusted so that the site was now on U.S. land. In subsequent years, the new fort, now named Fort Montgomery, was begun. It was occupied, although mostly by token forces, until 1908. Courtesy of the Clinton County Historical Museum

A military band from the Plattsburgh Barracks prepares to entertain guests in a bucolic scene at Hotel Champlain before it burned down in 1910. Courtesy of the Clinton County Historical Museum

Chapter 7

1900-1910

The twentieth century was ushered in with a grand winter carnival. Snow was abundant, although not in the quantity of the 1888 blizzard. The lake was solidly frozen over—and a good thing, too. Both snow and ice were necessary components of the winter carnival which started off with a wild hockey match between Plattsburgh and Malone, followed by an exhibition of fancy and trick skating by Miss Minnie Cummings and Mr. John Nilsson. The finale for the first day was a children's dress carnival parade.

On the second day Lake Champlain was the scene of an exciting ice boat race. Onlookers cheered as their favorites sped across the lake. A grand parade at 11:30 that morning featured a band with decorated sleighs and floats. A blockhouse built of ice was stormed by one hundred men dressed as Indians while a similar number served as defenders of the fort. Fireworks ended the second day of the celebration.

The final day featured another hockey game, this time between Malone and Saranac. Then spectators watched an ice skating ballet. Last of all was horse racing, featuring trotters and pacers on a one-half mile track.

The Lozier Company started a highly successful boat building concern in Plattsburgh in 1900. Their boats were sleek, expensive and desirable. However, when the Lozier car, a luxury car in every sense of the word, was produced in 1904, it was the epitome in one driver's words "of what a motor car should be. A Mercedes, a Locomobile, Pierce Arrow—I wouldn't trade a Lozier for any of them." Two Lozier cars, one with a four and one with a six cylinder engine, easily won the 1908 race on Brighton Beach, coming in first and second. The victory, the first of many that Lozier achieved, was celebrated back in Plattsburgh with the Lozier band parading through the factory. In 1910 the Lozier was the undisputed world champion. For eight years it produced cars that sold for more than five thousand dollars. With a labor force of four hundred men, the company had to work hard to fill the orders that came in from Europe and the United States. But the advent of lower-priced cars eventually forced the Lozier Company into bankruptcy in 1914. Today, antique car buffs will tell you that Lozier is on the list of the ten most desirable antique cars.

Plattsburgh Village was growing. It now encompassed land to the south of the village, including the Barracks. Worried over increasing expenses and work that needed to be done on proper sewage treatment, citizens approached the state legislature and in 1902 Plattsburgh became a city. The first mayor was Albert Sharron. Six aldermen, one from each of the six city wards, were also elected. Local pride in the new status of a city was high.

In Rouses Point, the eel boats were still making their way to New York City. These were curious vessels. The bottom of each boat held a screened section where eels

The Lozier Company sponsored a baseball team, photographed here in 1907. Courtesy of the Clinton County Historical Museum

The famous Lozier car made in Plattsburgh was probably beyond the means of most folks, but a member of the Patnode family is equally proud of his small jalopy.
  Photograph of Lozier car courtesy of Special Collections, Feinberg Library, SUNY, Plattsburgh.
  Patnode photograph courtesy of Addie L. Shields

This formal portrait of Alice Trainer Miner was painted by Lucile S. Dalrymple. Mrs. Miner, wife of the Chazy philanthropist William H. Miner, gave the village its colonial collection. Courtesy of Special Collections, Feinberg Library, SUNY, Plattsburgh

William H. Miner of Chazy was a local philanthropist. Courtesy of the Clinton County Historical Museum

were kept fresh during the journey. Lake Champlain eels were considered a particular delicacy in the finest restaurants in New York City. Apparently it was a profitable business.

About forty persons were stricken with smallpox in 1902. There was also a fire on Margaret Street that same year that threatened many buildings. Firemen, aided by Barracks soldiers, managed to get it under control.

In 1905 and 1906 the road through Beekmantown was macadamized. One hundred Italian workers hand shoveled the road bed and the banks. Twelve teams of horses carried crushed stone over which the surface would be finally poured. Route 9 was still a dirt road, but gradually macadam roads appeared in the city and outlying areas.

In Chazy William Miner had come back to his home territory—now a very wealthy man due to his inventions, which included the Miner Tandem Draft Rigging used on railroad cars and a patent for friction draft gear for use on heavier railroad cars and locomotives. Mr. Miner was born in Wisconsin, but he became an orphan and went to live with his aunt and uncle in Chazy. He was educated in a one-room schoolhouse that still stands on Miner property. Soon after the turn of the century, he and his wife, Alice, began to develop the 144-acre family farm into a model of scientific farming, known as Heart's Delight Farm. Eventually, they added sixteen thousand acres to the property. Using water from the Chazy River and Tracy Brook, he built a complete hydroelectric system supplying each building on the farm. From 1907 until 1922 he supplied electricity to Chazy Village. The Miner Foundation provided power for street lights until 1961. From 1908 until 1934 the only fire fighting equipment for the village was at Heart's Delight Farm. And as well as breeding and producing horses, cattle, sheep, pigs, poultry and squab, Miner stocked the ponds and Lake Alice (created by a series of concrete dams) with trout and black bass. His interest also included a game preserve of over one-thousand acres that housed buffalo, antelope, an Indian sacred cow, deer, elk, and partridge.

He employed many Chazy residents, and the impact was great in this small village. He also gave Chazy a new school—Chazy Rural School—the first consolidated school in New York State. Mr. Miner not only built the

Heart's Delight Farm in Chazy is viewed from the air. Here William Miner practiced scientific farming in all its aspects. Courtesy of Special Collections, Feinberg Library, SUNY, Plattsburgh

The Alice T. Miner Colonial Collection in Chazy is a popular museum which was masterminded by Mrs. William H. Miner, wife of the philanthropist. Courtesy of Special Collections, Feinberg Library, SUNY, Plattsburgh

school but paid the expenses for the building and equipment and covered the cost of transportation for students living within a certain distance from the school. It was a model building, praised highly by Gov. Alfred Smith who inspected the building in 1922.

Another gift to Chazy was the Alice T. Miner Collection, a museum in a house built in 1810 and restored by Mrs. Miner in 1924. It contains antique furniture, glass, silver, china, and many historical documents. Known locally as the Alice T. Miner Colonial Museum, it is open to the public.

Mr. Miner died in 1930. Heart's Delight Farm is now the William T. Miner Agricultural Institute and is connected to the State University at Plattsburgh.

He is remembered for his many philanthropies such as the Physicians' Hospital in Plattsburgh, the Kent-Delord House Museum, as well as the central school and museum in Chazy. He was a man of strong convictions and left a lasting legacy to Chazy.

Mooers Village was a prosperous place. In addition to the other factories and retail businesses, there was the Sheffield Excelsior Mill which used wood from poplar trees. This was then baled and shipped from the village until 1920.

In 1903 Mooers acquired a telephone exchange and in 1904 the village raised six thousand dollars by taxation for electric power. The plant was completed in 1930, assisted by the efforts of Assemblyman Wallace Knapp, who later became a New York State senator from this area. Incandescent street lights were installed and thirty homes wired for electricity. As late as 1920 the power was turned on for lighting at 4:00 p.m. every day and turned off in the

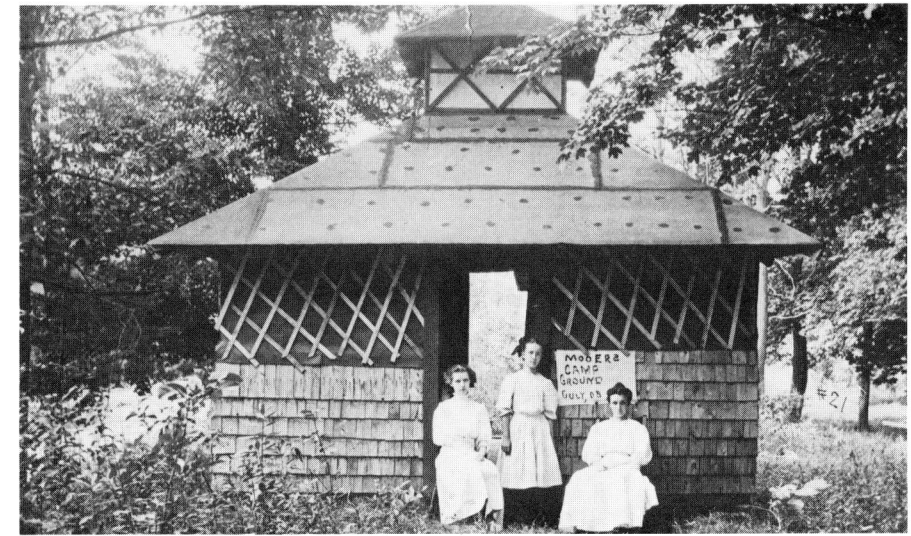

One of the many structures at the Mooers Camp Meeting grounds is shown here in the early twentieth century. The Camp Meeting Association still exists today. Courtesy of Special Collections, Feinberg Library, SUNY, Plattsburgh

The pulp mill owned by the J. and J. Rogers Company used this conveyer belt to pull the wood toward the enormous cooker which converted the wood into pulp. The company used wood from their own land holdings until lumber resources were exhausted. Eventually, wood for pulp was brought in from Canada by rail. Courtesy of the Clinton County Historical Museum

morning. (There was no power for lights during the day.)

Also, in 1903 the Mooers Camp Meeting Association was formed, partly as the result of Bushrod Sheddon Taylor's efforts. Mr. Taylor was a graduate of Wesleyan University. He joined the Joint Conference of the Methodist Church in 1877, and he and his wife served as missionaries in Panama and South America. He then came to Mooers to live and became a noted evangelist. The Camp Meeting Association picked a site of fifty acres between Mooers and Mooers Forks. A tent was used for the first meetings; permanent buildings followed and the Association still survives.

By 1905 the popularity of automobile travel made William Sweet of Chazy think of operating an auto ferry across the lake. He bought land and loaded stones from his own farm for a dock foundation at Chazy Landing. He also built a dock on Isle La Motte. He received authority from the state to operate the ferry, and in 1905 started business with the first gas-powered ferry named *The Twins*—in honor of his sons Clinton and Gerald. The ferry was sixty feet long and fourteen feet wide, with two double cylinder gasoline engines.

Early in the twentieth century the J. and J. Rogers Company of Au Sable Forks changed from mining iron to manufacturing pulp and paper. By 1902 they were making high quality paper and had moved the company offices to the paper mill. In 1905 the company also purchased Alice Falls Chasm with fifty thousand acres of timber.

On April 22, 1908 Chapter 149, an act providing for the tercentenary celebration of Lake Champlain's discovery, (the appointment of a commission prescribing its powers and duties and making an appropriation), passed the New York State Legislature, was signed by the governor, and became law. Negotiations with Vermont and Quebec, Canada, were conducted to insure that a suitable memorial to Samuel de Champlain was erected. Hugh

The Samuel de Champlain Monument, located at the mouth of the Saranac River, was designed by Hugh McLellan and dedicated at the tercentenary celebration in 1909. Courtesy of Special Collections, Feinberg Library, SUNY, Plattsburgh

McLellan was commissioned to design a permanent monument in Plattsburgh. July 4-10, 1909 was set aside to commemorate this historic event, and what a celebration it was! Dignitaries included President William Howard Taft; Secretary of War Jacob M. Dickinson; Governor Hughes; the Rt. Hon. James Bryce, British ambassador; the Hon. J. J. Jusserand, the French ambassador; and Hon. Rodolphe Lemieux, postmaster general of Canada. The United States Navy sent the torpedo boat *Manley* and two steam cutters *Plattsburgh* and the *Burlington* to join in the festivities. This was the first naval exhibition on the lake since the War of 1812. Part of the celebration was an historic reenactment of Champlain discovering the lake and Champlain's battle with the Iroquois, and Hiawatha, reputed organizer of the five nations. A floating island was constructed for this occasion; 168 Iroquois provided the entertainment. Traveling up and down both sides of the lake, this island with its Indian inhabitants delighted spectators.

This was the program for July 7, 1909:
Bi-State Programme
Wednesday, July 7, 1909-Plattsburgh, NY
 9:45 a.m. - Address by the President at Cliff Haven
10:30 a.m. - Indian Pageants at Mouth of Saranac River, Plattsburgh
10:30 a.m. - Private Reception by the President for the Representatives of foreign governments and members of the New York Legislature at Hotel Champlain.
12:30 p.m. - Luncheon
 1:30 p.m. - Special Train, Hotel Champlain for Plattsburgh Barracks.

Clinton Hall at the corner of Margaret and Clinton streets in Plattsburgh was decorated for the Champlain Valley Tercentenary July 4-11, 1909. Courtesy of the Clinton County Historical Museum

Trinity Square and Clinton County Courthouse, Plattsburgh are dressed in red, white and blue bunting for the tercentenary in 1909. Courtesy of the Clinton County Historical Museum

2:00 p.m. - Parade and Review of Military, Civic and Fraternal Organizations at Plattsburgh Barracks
3:30 p.m. - Literary Exercises at Plattsburgh Barracks, including brief addresses by
President William Howard Taft
The Hon. J. J. Jusserand, The French Ambassador
Rt. Hon. James Bryce, the British Ambassador
Hon. Rodolphe Lemieux, Postmaster-General of Canada
A Formal Historical Address, entitled "The Iroquois and the Struggle for America," by the Hon. Elihu Root, U.S. Senator from New York
An Original Poem, entitled, "Champlain and Lake Champlain," by Daniel L. Cady of New York.
5:00 p.m. - Evening Parade at Plattsburgh Barracks
7:45 p.m. - Indian Pageants at Mouth of Saranac River, Plattsburgh
8:00 p.m. - Banquet for the President at Hotel Champlain, with post-prandial speeches by the President, Vice-President, and distinguished guests.

Dr. Joseph Henri LaRocque's home and office at 66 Oak Street were lavishly decorated for the Champlain Valley Tercentenary, July 4-9, 1909. Dr. LaRocque was born in Quebec, and came to Plattsburgh in 1848, where he served as a village trustee for six years in addition to his medical practice. Courtesy of the Clinton County Historical Museum

Historical re-enactments were favorite themes in parades. An elaborate Beekmantown float, drawn by four elaborately decorated horses, caught the attention of onlookers waiting for the rest of the parade in 1909. Courtesy of Addie Shields, Clinton County Historian

Coon's ice cream delivery wagon passes in front of the courthouse during the tercentenary celebration in July 1909. Courtesy of the Clinton County Historical Museum

A large crowd turned out for the parade with historical floats celebrating the Champlain Valley Tercentenary in 1909. The parade is winding down Bridge Street in Plattsburgh. Courtesy of the Clinton County Historical Museum

9:00 p.m. - Fireworks at Mouth of Saranac River, Plattsburgh

In May 1910, while preparations were begun for the season, Hotel Champlain at Bluff Point burned to the ground. Cottages and a building that could serve as a restaurant were still intact. These were rented for the summer months.

By August of the same year plans for a new hotel were under way and it was completed in 1911, just as luxuriously appointed as the old one but with a large garage added, plus many new amenities for people arriving at the hotel by car. It was decorated in the style of Louis XVI, but with all the modern conveniences and equipment. Once more the wealthy and the famous flocked to its doors.

The first hospital in Clinton County was the Champlain Valley Hospital, a nonsectarian hospital run by the Grey Nuns of the Sacred Heart. A nursing school also opened at that time. A fundraising campaign to build and maintain the new hospital was successful and now, at last, doctors had a place to which they could send their patients.

Clinton County always had newspapers, some of which had a long span of existence, others which lasted only a brief time. In the first decade of the twentieth century there were four weekly papers: *Plattsburgh Evening News* (1900-1915); the *Plattsburgh Sentinel* (1857-1931); *Plattsburgh Press* (1894-1942), and the *Plattsburgh Republican* (1811-1916). In 1916 it became a daily paper and changed its name to *Plattsburgh Daily Republican*. The *Rouses Point Times* and the *Adirondack Record* were also among those being published.

A construction crew lines up in front of the new Hotel Champlain, built after a disastrous fire burned the original hotel to the ground on May 28, 1910. Courtesy of the Clinton County Historical Museum

Shown here is the cornerstone laying for the Champlain Valley Hospital in Plattsburgh in 1910. Courtesy of the Clinton County Historical Museum

The staff of the Lakeside Press in Rouses Point was photographed in 1910 with the tools of their trade and a magnificent stove. Courtesy of Craig Koste

William A. Howell III looks calmly out at the world from his seat on a pony cart. Courtesy of the Clinton County Historical Museum

119

The horse-drawn Hotel Champlain bus conveys guests to the hotel, followed by a pleasure wagon and a lone bicyclist. Courtesy of the Clinton County Historical Museum

Passengers are bound for a summer trip on the railroad circa 1900. The station house in background is at Chazy Lake. Courtesy of Special Collections, Feinberg Library, SUNY, Plattsburgh

A family outing through the Saranac Valley in a pleasure wagon conjures up an era of unhurried pastimes. Courtesy of Craig Koste

The Clinton County Board of Supervisors is pictured here from 1900. Courtesy of the Clinton County Historical Museum

Early streetscapes provide invaluable information about the locations of buildings. This view of Margaret Street, Plattsburgh, also shows the recently laid trolley tracks and various forms of transportation in 1900. Courtesy of the Clinton County Historical Museum

Clinton County Agricultural Society Fair Grounds were located on Bailey Avenue in Plattsburgh in 1900. Courtesy of the Clinton County Historical Museum

In this photograph, the 1901 Plattsburgh High School football team seems determined to frighten away any adversaries and win by intimidation. Courtesy of the Clinton County Historical Museum

The former Plattsburgh High School was a stately building on the corner of Oak and Brinkerhoff streets where the public library is located now. The graduating class of 1902 was among the first to emerge into the brave new world of the twentieth century. Courtesy of the Clinton County Historical Museum

Here we see the interior of the Rouses Point Post Office in 1902. There are lots of cubbyholes for the mail to be sorted and held for the villagers. Courtesy of Craig Koste

Families tended to be large in the early part of the twentieth century. Here Michael J. Halligan, postmaster of Rouses Point in 1902, (seated, second from left), poses proudly with his wife, children and grandchildren. Courtesy of Mary G. Leggett

The following quote is from the C. B. Hancock diary, August 1, 1903: "This was a clear bright day and it was a bad day for the railroad. The freight train came from Rouses Point at half past nine o'clock this morning, and the bridge was open for Jim Averill boat and the engine and twelve cars went in the river and the fireman went with the engine and drowned. The engineer jumped off. The engineer's name was Homer Elittle. Thare [sic] was two cars of stock and some four or five cows and calves got out alive. It was a big sight to see. The bridge was nocked [sic] off in the river and Ed Lapoint was station agent and bridge tender, and was on the bridge when this hapened [sic] but was not hurt." Courtesy of Special Collections, Feinberg Library, SUNY, Plattsburgh

F. M. Purdy operated a general store and a mill at Altona. The store no longer exists, but other buildings on the property have been lovingly preserved. Courtesy of Mr. & Mrs. C. Randall Beach

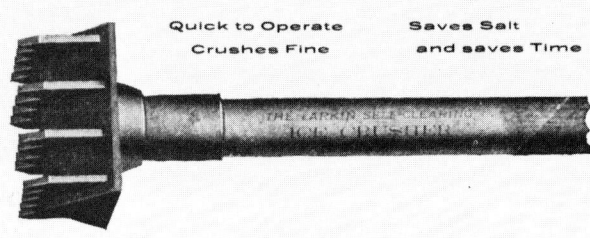

Otis Larkin, owner of a drugstore in Plattsburgh, was a man of vision according to this advertisement for the Larkin ice crusher, one of the "new-fangled" inventions of the early twentieth century. Courtesy of the Clinton County Historical Museum

A photograph of the St. Jean-Baptiste Society, a Catholic organization dedicated to the mutual benefit of its members, was taken in front of St. Peter's School in Plattsburgh. Courtesy of the Clinton County Historical Museum

Keziah Bull Kimball stands outside her modest board and batten house at Pickett's Corners in Saranac. Courtesy of the Clinton County Historical Museum

The Danis block of grey stone tenement apartments was located at Cornelia Street, Plattsburgh between North Catherine and Oak streets. Courtesy of the Clinton County Historical Museum

Posing for a photograph at the Boomhower Grocery Store in Mooers, from left to right, are: Frendy Barney, unidentified seated man, John LaFave, William Eddy, Anselm Goodrich, Orma Sheffield, Electa Corkins (Mrs. Henry Davidson), Frank Goodrich, M. Corkins, Billy Brickey (seated), Hattie Wilson, Margaret Lamberton (Mrs. Elmer), Earl Keith, Sam Bates, Dud Coakley, and little Earl Wilson. Those sitting on the step are not identified. Courtesy of the Clinton County Historical Museum

A turn-of-the-century photograph of Dawson's Store in Beekmantown shows a typical country store interior. It subsequently became Rea's Store. Courtesy of Special Collections, Feinberg Library, SUNY, Plattsburgh

Frank Harrison Graves owned and operated a well-known grocery store at 15 Bridge Street, Plattsburgh at the intersection of Bridge and River streets, formerly known as "Guibord's Corner" because Guibord's Grocery Store was located there. Courtesy of the Clinton County Historical Museum

The Redford picnic is in progress, where the men gathered in 1907 to place wagers on their favorite horses. This annual affair on August 15 has been a tradition of many years' standing in Clinton County. Courtesy of the Clinton County Historical Museum

Some Plattsburgh citizens stand on the piazza of the Young Men's Christian Association's building in 1908. Modernization of the building took place in 1963. Courtesy of the Clinton County Historical Museum

The McGaulley family was photographed in 1908. It was typical of Irish or French families of this period to have a daughter who took the veil and became a nun. Courtesy of the Clinton County Historical Museum

Winter in Champlain brings out the horse-drawn sleighs for transportation circa 1908. Courtesy of Special Collections, Feinberg Library, SUNY, Plattsburgh

Two intrepid hunters pose with guns at the ready and dinner already hanging from one of the barrels! Courtesy of Special Collections, Feinberg Library, SUNY, Plattsburgh

Baseball was a keen spectator sport in Dannemora in 1909. Courtesy of Craig Koste

People wait for their mail at the Redford Post Office in 1910. Courtesy of Special Collections, Feinberg Library, SUNY, Plattsburgh

The interior of the Myers and Belden Grocery Store located at 103 Margaret Street, Plattsburgh shows a typical shop around 1910. Courtesy of the Clinton County Historical Museum

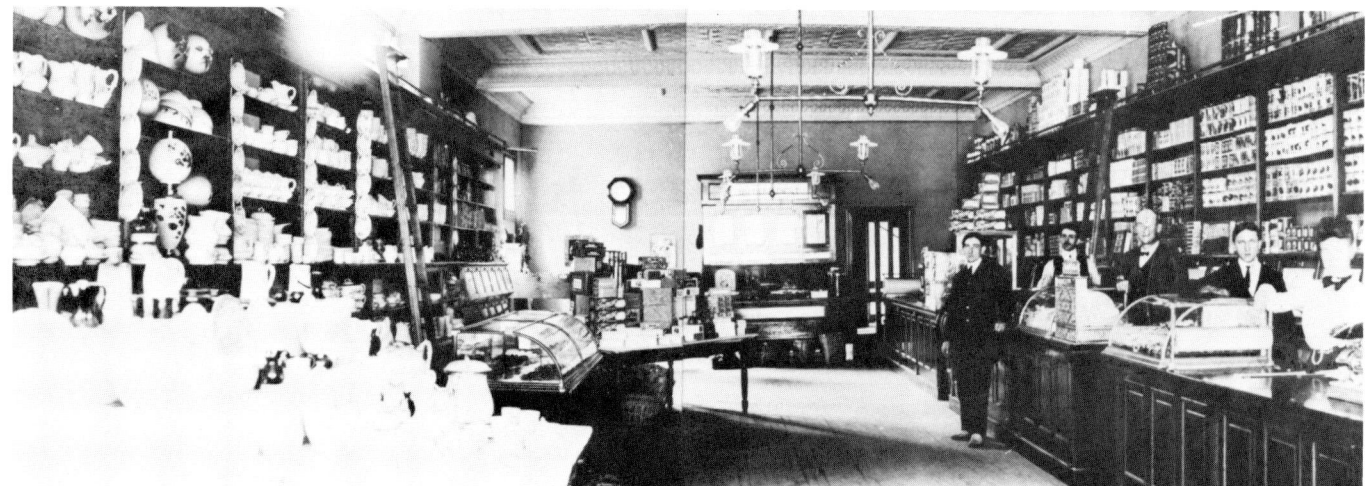

Chazy's Main Street wears an idyllic appearance in 1910. Courtesy of Special Collections, Feinberg Library, SUNY, Plattsburgh

Joseph Fountain (born in 1845) and his dog Jack stand on the porch of Fountain's grocery store at 104 Montcalm Avenue, Plattsburgh. His grandson Joseph ("Pete" Fountain II) is holding the horse in front. Courtesy of Norma Fountain

The following were graduates of Plattsburgh High School in 1910: Silas Clark, Raymond Prime, Leo Lyons, William Mason, Ralph Brown, Clifford Day, Paul Clay, Hubert Jerry, William Kelly, Arthur Sharron, Everett Corrigan, Leo Gauthier, Elkins Dale, Terry Curtis, Bertol Merrihew, Charles Harrington, LeRoy Hyde, Florence Nightengale, Julia Clark, Diantha Lapham, Jean Purdy, Marjorie Lansing, Mabel Dominy, Mary Kavanaugh, Frances Baker, Marion Chasnier, and Helen McDougall. Courtesy of the Clinton County Historical Museum

Section V
Wars and Depression

Everyone is watching intently while the sergeant in charge instructs a rather uncertain soldier in the intricacies of a machine gun. Courtesy of the Clinton County Historical Museum

Chapter 8

1910-1920

A huge fire in Champlain in 1912 endangered the entire community, owing to a wind almost like a tornado. Starting in the building across from the Village Hall, it quickly spread to nearby buildings, crossed the river and destroyed most structures in its path. The most grievous loss was the Pliny Moore mansion, built in 1800. Fire departments came from Rouses Point and Plattsburgh, and a special train started from Malone with equipment, but turned back after receiving news that the fire was contained.

A commission was appointed by New York state to celebrate the centennial of the Battle of Lake Champlain from September 6 to 11, 1914. Among the distinguished members of this commission were Francis Lynde Stetson, chairman; Thomas F. Conway, vice chairman; Charles J. Vert, secretary; and Franklin Delano Roosevelt, who was then the assistant secretary of the Navy. One hundred twenty-five thousand dollars was appropriated by the state to place permanent markers at historic sites. Washington, D.C., matched this amount for the purpose of placing a permanent memorial to the victory of Macdonough and Macomb. Historic markers were erected at Forts Brown, Moreau, and Scott; Pike's Cantonment; Dead Creek Bridge; Riverside Cemetery; Salmon River Road, and the Brick Tavern.

Plattsburgh decked itself out for this occasion. Red, white, and blue bunting adorned the houses and business section, and celebrants thronged the street to watch the parade. At Plattsburgh Barracks *The Pageant of the Champlain Valley*, written by Margaret Maclaren Eager, was presented on four separate occasions—Tuesday, September 8 at 8:00 p.m.; Wednesday, September 9 at 3:00 p.m.; Thursday, September 10 at 8:00 p.m., and Friday, September 11 at 10:00 a.m. The official program lists many prominent Plattsburgh citizens who reenacted those famous personages of our early history. The centennial celebration of 1914 marked a singular event in the history of Clinton County.

In 1914 Europe was at war. In Plattsburgh an idea conceived by Maj. Gen. Leonard Wood began to take form. General Wood believed that every citizen owed a military obligation to his country during wartime. This belief was the basis of the "Plattsburgh Idea."

The sinking of the *Lusitania* on May 7, 1915 hastened its fulfillment. According to the War Department General Order No. 38 on June 22, 1915, young businessmen paid their own way to Plattsburgh to receive military training in anticipation of America's entry into the war. Their training was intense and well planned. A typical day included 5:45 a.m. reveille, calisthenics and drill, lunch, then specialized instruction in signal corps, cavalry, engineering, or artillery. On Wednesday, August 25, 1915, Col. Teddy Roosevelt arrived in Plattsburgh to address the troops. The reverberation from that visit rocked the White House and

Francis Lynde Stetson was the chairman of the commission appointed by the state of New York to celebrate the centennial of the Battle of Lake Champlain in 1914. Courtesy of the Clinton County Historical Museum

Willingness to serve in the army is the patriotic theme of this illustration for sheet music published during World War I. Courtesy of Mayor and Mrs. Carlton E. Rennell

Major General Wood's career. After Colonel Roosevelt addressed the troops, he spoke to reporters at the Delaware and Hudson depot just before his departure. The *New York Times* headline ran "Roosevelt would back the President only if right; if wrong he says at Plattsburgh Camp citizens should show him his duty." However, training went on despite much debate.

Pittsburgh (PA) Gazette Times ran this article: "August 21, 1916—At Plattsburgh twenty-five rookies were victims of the heat today. The mercury was above 110 degrees all day. Company combats took up the morning, the men remaining on the rifle range where conditions were unusually bad. Maj. Gen. Leonard Wood announced that rookies who desired to take the exams for the volunteer officer corps could do so after the present encampment. The general is anxious that a large percentage of the men qualify. These rookies supplied their own uniforms, shoes—all equipment except guns and ammunition."

Then the Selective Service Act of May 1917 became effective and the Plattsburgh Idea was vindicated. America was at war and trained men were ready for combat. Today there are markers in many local villages listing the brave lads who marched off to the "war to end all wars" and gave their last full measure for their country.

As if war were not enough, a flu epidemic struck Clinton County in 1917 devastating the population.

Among the people of this decade who made a singular impact on Clinton County, indeed on its surrounding counties, were the Barton physicians. Dr. Lyman Guy Barton was the son of the pioneer physician, Dr. Lyman Barton, who practiced for many years in Willsboro. Dr. Lyman Guy Barton first studied mechanical engineering at Cornell and then switched to medicine at Dartmouth. He practiced in Willsboro until his busy surgical schedule at the Champlain Valley Hospital in Plattsburgh necessitated moving his family to the city in 1914. For over twenty-five years he made house calls and performed operations in kitchens. His background in engineering and his skill as a surgeon combined in his development of new instruments for surgery. He developed skull tongs, traction frames, and other surgical instruments. Perhaps the Bar-

A magnificent celebration took place to mark the centennial of the Battle of Lake Champlain. On September 11, 1914, a parade on Bridge Street is watched by an enthusiastic crowd. Courtesy of the Clinton County Historical Museum

A Schuyler Falls float in the Battle of Lake Champlain centennial parade showed that protection of the citizenry was in good hands. Courtesy of Craig Koste

The Fifth U.S. Infantry band avoided striking a wrong note by having its mascot on hand, at left. This photograph was taken at the Plattsburgh Military Barracks. Courtesy of the Clinton County Historical Museum

Col. Theodore (Teddy) Roosevelt chats with Maj. Gen. Leonard Wood at the Plattsburgh Military Barracks in 1915. Courtesy of the Clinton County Historical Museum

ton forceps—used in obstetrics—was his most famous invention, used by prominent surgeons throughout the United States, Canada, and Europe. These forceps brought a significant decrease in infant and maternal mortality. He had two sons, Dr. Lyman Guy Barton, Jr., and Dr. Philip Barton, both of whom served the community for over forty years each.

Loyal F. Smith was a man whose generosity to the city was remarkable in a different way. The organization of YMCA Building Club earlier in the century resulted in the purchase of a mansion on the corner of Brinkerhoff and Oak streets. A twenty-day campaign netted twenty thousand dollars, which Mr. Smith matched and added to later. Loyal Smith left money in his will for a badly needed city

A Cadillac armoured car and Red Cross ambulance are about to be driven from Plattsburgh to New York City for shipment to the front during World War I. Courtesy of the Clinton County Historical Museum

hall. John Russell Pope, a noted American architect, was selected for the job. The imposing structure, crowned by a gilded dome, was ready for use in 1918.

In Au Sable Forks, the Adirondack Granite company was formed at a cost of one million dollars. It took over the Au Sable Forks Granite Company and all stockholders of that company were given additional stock as bonuses. In 1913 the Champlain Green Company came into existence and established a plant on the Bailey property in Au Sable Forks. An unusual dark green granite was mined from this land. William Carnes and his son, Fred, prospected and opened several quarries in Au Sable, as well as a finishing plant.

Entertainment during this period included dancing at Red Leonard's Hall on Margaret Street in Plattsburgh, sleigh rides, skating, and ice boating in the winter, picnicking, auto touring, and lake excursions in the summer. Charles Hudson had organized the Philharmonic Champlain Choral Union, which offered concerts with the Plattsburgh Symphony Orchestra. Redpath Chautauqua came each summer.

The Redpath Chautauqua tent became a welcome summer sight in Plattsburgh during this decade, continuing well into the 1920s. It brought with it moral lectures and a variety of entertainment for children and adults. Grand operas such as *Faust,* a Victor Herbert musical comedy, impersonations and a Highland Band were typical fare for the Chautauqua week.

Military preparedness is evident in a photograph of Plattsburgh City Hall. Courtesy of Special Collections, Feinberg Library, SUNY, Plattsburgh

A postcard depicts actress Mabel Normand's visit to the Plattsburgh Barracks. Miss Normand was one of Mack Sennett's bathing beauties and later starred with Charlie Chaplin in the Keystone Film Company motion pictures. Courtesy of Special Collections, Feinberg Library, SUNY, Plattsburgh

"Over there, Over there. Send the word. Send the word to beware." Words from a George M. Cohan song seem to reflect the mood of these World War I trainees as they practice on a dummy of Admiral Von Tirpitz, the German Naval minister. Courtesy of the Clinton County Historical Museum

Three World War I army dandies are dressed in what was obviously handed to them directly from the shelf without regard for sizes. Courtesy of the Clinton County Historical Museum

A patriotic street rally marked the end of the third Liberty Loan drive in Plattsburgh in May 1918. A raised sign indicates that the drive raised over $22,000, exceeding its goal. Courtesy of Special Collections, Feinberg Library, SUNY, Plattsburgh

Privates Thomas McDonough and J. F. Griffith from Plattsburgh with the 101st Regiment, 26th Division prepare the bread ration in France during World War I. Courtesy of Special Collections, Feinberg Library, SUNY, Plattsburgh

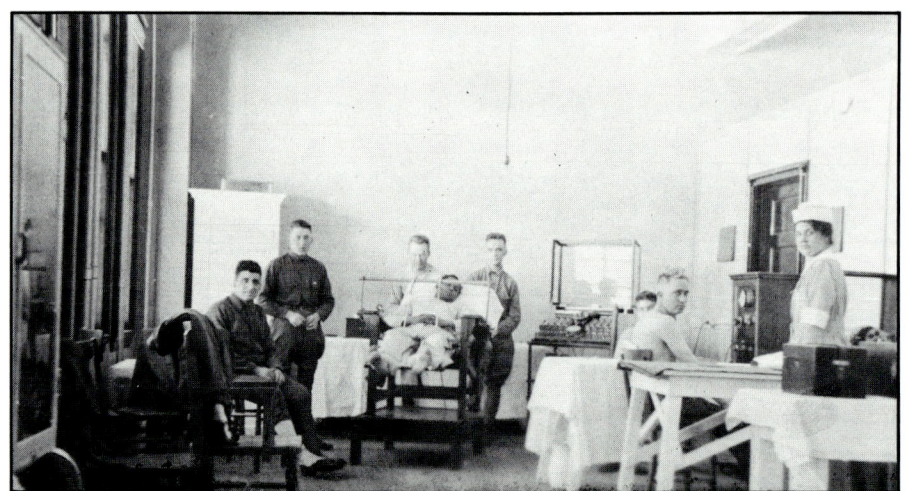

Medicine was still somewhat primitive during World War I, but soldiers received the best treatment available. Courtesy of Special Collections, Feinberg Library, SUNY, Plattsburgh

The Wilcox Dock in Plattsburgh was apparently a favorite mooring place for small pleasure craft. Courtesy of Special Collections, Feinberg Library, SUNY, Plattsburgh

Canal boats, which were the workhorses of Lake Champlain's maritime trade, are moored at Rouses Point. This photograph was taken by Frank Pardy, a Rouses Point merchant and ardent amateur photographer. Courtesy of the Clinton County Historical Museum

The present site of City Hall, Plattsburgh, was once a residential and commercial area. Prominent in this 1910 photograph is the church where all Catholics worshipped prior to the establishment of St. Peter's (the French church) and St. John's (the Irish church). This church and all other structures on each side of the street were demolished to make way for City Hall and the Macdonough Monument. Courtesy of the Clinton County Historical Museum

Hotel Chateaugay at Lyon Mountain was operated by the Chateaugay Ore and Iron Company. This picture taken about 1910 shows the first floor restaurant and other dining facilities. Courtesy of the Clinton County Historical Museum

A steamroller and other equipment for road surfacing are shown in this early twentieth century view of Rouses Point. Courtesy of Craig Koste

The Meserve family and their friends were photographed on Crab Island at the monument which honors the men killed in the battles of Valcour (1776) and Plattsburgh (1814). Courtesy of the Clinton County Historical Museum

Alvin L. Inman was an architect who designed most of the English Tudor houses to be seen in Clinton County. When this photograph was taken, he was a member of the Board of Directors of the Plattsburgh National Bank and Trust Company. Courtesy of Special Collections, Feinberg Library, SUNY, Plattsburgh

The Lake Champlain Association held a splendid banquet at the Waldorf-Astoria Hotel in New York City in 1912, attended by a delegation from the people of France. Courtesy of the Clinton County Historical Museum

Vacationers, c. 1910, on the dock of Hotel Champlain. The original hotel is in the background, and Singing Sands Beach on the right. Courtesy of the Clinton County Historical Museum

Musicians tune up for the evening's entertainment at Hotel Champlain around 1913. Courtesy of Special Collections, Feinberg Library, SUNY, Plattsburgh

Lt.-Gov. Thomas F. Conway (third from right) is one of the secular dignitaries arriving at the Catholic Summer School of America. Courtesy of Special Collections, Feinberg Library, SUNY, Plattsburgh

Enthusiastic supporters stand in the background as Plattsburgh High School baseball players have their picture taken in 1914 at the ballpark located on the northeast corner of Bailey Avenue and Oak Street. Courtesy of the Clinton County Historical Museum

The Suburban Transportation Company bus is parked in front of Sanborn and Bartle, optometrists, 44 Clinton Street, Plattsburgh. William A. Hallock was the manager in 1913. Courtesy of the Clinton County Historical Museum

Farmers (John Doakes, Jim Shields and Bill Soper) were bringing in the hay on the Shields farm in Beekmantown. Courtesy of Addie L. Shields

Pictured are Marshall Bilow, Emma (Dupree) Bilow, Edith Bilow, and Andrew Bilow at their farm in Ellenburgh. Courtesy of Special Collections, Feinberg Library, SUNY, Plattsburgh

In a photograph that illustrates the transition between horse-drawn wagons and motorized vehicles, both drivers are ready to make delivery of completed laundry. Behind them employees of the Plattsburgh Steam Laundry are lined up. Andrew F. Williams was the proprietor. *Courtesy of the Clinton County Historical Museum*

The Palace Theatre located on the east side of North River Street advertised the coolest spot in Plattsburgh. Later this structure and the others on this street were demolished to make room for the Macdonough Monument. *Courtesy of Special Collections, Feinberg Library, SUNY, Plattsburgh*

Constructed in 1915, Chazy Central Rural School was the first centralized rural school in New York State. Horse-drawn school buses picked up students and brought them to school. In the 1970s this building was torn down to make room for a new school. Courtesy of the Clinton County Historical Museum

A train wreck happened at Champlain on March 30, 1916, near the milk plant. Courtesy of Mr. and Mrs. Harold Smith

The railroad station at Valcour was a favorite spot for young people to hitch a train ride to school in Plattsburgh. In this photograph workmen and supervisors engaged in building additions to the Jonas Platt house await the next train. Courtesy of Special Collections, Feinberg Library, SUNY, Plattsburgh

Prominent businessmen posed for this photo at O'Donnell's Store in Peru. Standing from the left are Albert Mason, Frank Finney, John Booth, Harry Bosworth, Will Mason, George Gove, Leighton Bartlett, Herbert Mason, Edward Mason, Charles Mason, Henry Macomber, Fred Bosworth, George Mason, and Charles O'Donnell. Seated are Matthew Mason and Gary McGee. Courtesy of the Clinton County Historical Museum

Mr. Saunders's route went as far as Keeseville from Peru, selling and delivering meats and groceries to housewives along the way. Courtesy of the Peru Free Library

Shown here is the interior of the Cady Drug Company, Plattsburgh, which was located on the corner of Margaret and Bridge streets in 1917.

Plattsburgh Traction company operated from 1895 to 1929. Plattsburgh's distinctive white-painted summer trolley cars were once a familiar sight on the city's streets and along the road to Bluff Point. Here is open car No. 12 at "Davis Corners," U.S. Avenue and Elizabeth Street, inbound from Bluff Point. As all regular cars went around the city belt line, the sign thus would be carried on the front fender until the car got back to Bluff Point, then changed to the opposite fender. Harry Miller, who in later years became general superintendent, is the conductor standing on the running board in this circa 1917 photo. *Courtesy of the Clinton County Historical Museum*

Plattsburgh's City Hall is a neoclassical building set in the heart of downtown. Designed by nationally-known architect John Russell Pope, the building was constructed in 1917-18, thanks to a large bequest from Loyal B. Smith. Looking over City Hall is the spire of Trinity Church, later removed for safety reasons. *Courtesy of the Clinton County Historical Museum*

A performance of Flora Bella *was the best casino musical show in years, according to the advertisement of August 15, 1917, that ran in the* Plattsburgh Daily Republican. *Courtesy of Susan Llewellyn*

World War I soldiers were photographed during maneuvers on the pine barrens. This area is now east of Route 22, south of Plattsburgh, in the general vicinity of the current Plattsburgh Air Force Base flight line. Courtesy of the Clinton County Historical Museum

Dr. Marnes' Marina, Rouses Point, is shown about 1918. Sleek inboard launches and flags fluttering in the breeze make a gay summer scene. Courtesy of the Clinton County Historical Museum

It's either shoot the car or the smiling passengers who don't seem to mind their unexpected stop on a country road. The gentleman on the right is either reaching for a gun or for a liquid restorative! Courtesy of the Clinton County Historical Museum

This handsome building on the corner of Oak and Clinton streets was erected in 1885 as the headquarters of the Chateaugay Ore and Iron Company. It has been the Supreme Court Library for many years. In the photograph, circa 1920, the original Baptist Church can be seen on the left and a corner of the roof of the Plattsburgh Theatre on the right. Courtesy of Special Collections, Feinberg Library, SUNY, Plattsburgh

Four ladies are ready for a ride in an automobile outside Frank Pardy's store in Rouses Point. Courtesy of the Clinton County Historical Museum

The Samuel Mendelsohn Store, at 30 River Street (now City Hall Place), was the last store next to the Macdonough Monument Park. Mendelsohn imported and sold fine whiskies. Prohibition put an end to many local businesses that dealt in liquors. Courtesy of the Clinton County Historical Museum

This is one of the historical buildings in Mooers Forks used as a mill in earlier days. Courtesy of Richard Ward

Chapter 9

1920-1930

The year was 1920. Congress had passed the Volstead Act over President Wilson's veto on October 27, 1919. On January 19, 1920 the law became effective. "Ain't We Got Fun," the title of a popular song of the day, seemed to reflect the nation's mood, and it was a feeling shared by many people in Clinton County. Quebec was wet, the United States was dry, and a rapidly growing business called bootlegging flourished. It was a time of tall tales and legends that are still told today—some true, some almost true—of shoot-outs and fast getaways. The highways, the lake, and the railroad all became avenues that the bootleggers used to transport their forbidden cargo.

Farmers who traditionally believed that less government was the best government found that there was a healthy profit in hiding bootleg booze on the farms. It provided a hedge against capricious Mother Nature and the vagaries of the farming industry. It was not unheard of for a border patrolman to find, under a haystack, a car filled with Mumm's extra dry champagne or packed in fish crates heading south by rail.

Congestion at the border became a common occurrence. Rouses Point, Champlain and Mooers, the border villages, were the scenes for many confrontations between border patrolmen and bootleggers. One story concerns "Father Bashaw," a pseudonym for a notorious bootlegger, who reversed his collar, posed as a priest, and drove his Cadillac loaded with Scotch across the border without incident. His relief was so great that he stopped at a local church to light a candle. While he was giving thanks, his car was searched and he was arrested as he left the church. The *Plattsburgh Daily Republican* of September 6, 1929, reported that 739 seizures had taken place at the Rouses Point Customs House during August. These included seven cars, and one freight train car of liquor and lumber.

For thirteen years Prohibition was the law of the land, but the nation's mood changed. The stock market crash had taken place, followed by the Great Depression. In 1933 the Volstead Act was repealed.

Clinton County's mood was very much the same as the rest of America's. Women won the vote in 1920, the war and rationing were over, and the ambiance was exhilarating. Bravely, women marched into barber shops and had their hair bobbed. Marcel waves were fashionable. Cloche hats hugged the shingled heads of stylish women. Hemlines were shorter and georgette evening dresses were short, trimmed with beads or fringe. The flapper was *in!* Women smoked and in winter wore their overshoes casually unbuckled.

There were many more cars in the county now and the roads were improving each year. Old-timers remember the big red Marmon touring cars with the jump seats in the back; the Buick touring cars were likewise

A United States marshal destroys liquor before a crowd of interested citizens at Rouses Point during the 1920s. Courtesy of Dr. Allan S. Everest

During Prohibition people could drive to the Meridian for a legal Canadian drink and dancing. It was a gathering place for locals and also for gangsters. Courtesy of Special Collections, Feinberg Library, SUNY, Plattsburgh

Customs agents at Rouses Point were kept busy during the Prohibition Era. Courtesy of Special Collections, Feinberg Library, SUNY, Plattsburgh

Robert O. Kellogg, son of Grace Olyphant Kellogg, sits in his mother's "Revere" car in 1922. It had a four cylinder, large-bore, long-stroke Dusenberg engine, four speeds forward, top speed 84 mph. It cost $5,200 and was faster than a "Stutz" or "Mercer." Courtesy of Special Collections, Feinberg Library, SUNY, Plattsburgh

An early traffic indicator at the corner of Margaret and Bridge streets in Plattsburgh shows the suggested route to Albany via Route 9 South. The First National Bank now occupies the site of Cady's Drugstore. Courtesy of Special Collections, Feinberg Library, SUNY, Plattsburgh

equipped and fitted with canvas and isinglass windows that snapped on the sides to protect passengers from sudden inclement weather. The more sedate drove a sedan, perhaps a Studebaker, with beige silk curtains that could be drawn over the side windows and crystal vases mounted on either side of the interior.

There were still bicycles in use and not just for kids. Men with their black lunch pails rode their bicycles to the mills. No one seeing them at that time would have guessed that within the next twenty-five years the income of that blue-collar worker would outstrip that of the white-collar worker, sedately and properly dressed, making his way to the office or the bank.

The Plattsburgh library was on the first floor of City Hall where Helen Hale presided over it. By now the book collection had been greatly enlarged and there was an excellent children's section, as well as a fine adult section which also featured bestsellers of the period.

The telephone company in Plattsburgh was located on Oak Street. An operator put through calls; direct dialing was still in the future. Other telephone exchanges were by now serving villages throughout the county.

On Wednesday evenings during summer most Plattsburghers drove to the Plattsburgh Barracks to hear concerts in the bandstand on the Oval. Cars were parked around the bandstand on the Barracks Oval; the military band played each number and people applauded by honking car horns vigorously. Small children ran among

Everybody went to the beach in 1924. The golden sands and the blue waters of Lake Champlain were an irresistible invitation to escape the heat. And they took their cars as well. Courtesy of the Clinton County Historical Museum

A gentlemen's putting match took place on the beautiful golf course overlooking Lake Champlain, which is the third oldest course in the country. Courtesy of the Clinton County Historical Museum

the parked cars and a splendid time was had by all.

Lectures and sessions at the Catholic Summer School were well attended by many people in the county, particularly nearby residents of Valcour, Peru, and Plattsburgh. Concerts and performances by solo artists were also offered by the Summer School. Hotel Champlain was still a focal point of attraction and one could see golfers in their plus fours on the course from early morning until dusk each day.

Family picnics, either in the country or at the beaches, occupied Sunday afternoons. Fare for a Sunday picnic in those days usually consisted of sliced chicken sandwiches and milk with homemade cake for dessert.

Radio had been invented by the 1920s and most

households owned one, with earphones and huge horn. Everyone gathered on Sunday evenings to listen to Jack Benny's comedy show. Fathers tended to like news reports and were delighted when odd quirks in the atmosphere brought in for a brief moment or two a station from as far away as Newark, New Jersey.

Women's bridge clubs and literary societies were popular. The oldest of these was the Tuesday Club, which began in 1892 as the Clover Club, was reorganized in 1896 as the Tuesday Club, and is still in existence in the 1980s. Another literary club in Plattsburgh began about 1913 and flourished until 1950. Almost every small town or village in the county boasted its own reading or literary group which met regularly.

People still watched election results being announced from the newspaper office on Clinton Street on election nights—and there were still torchlight parades held for victorious candidates. And as usual before election, candidates attended all church suppers they could.

The Young Women's League on the corner of Oak and Broad streets served as a place for girls and women to work and play together, sponsoring plays, Campfire Girls, and Brownie Scouts, as well as evening get-togethers. Service clubs came into existence during these years. The Rotary Club in Plattsburgh was started in 1926, Kiwanis in 1929, and the Lions' Club in the 1930s.

Parades and Fourth of July speeches were still a highlight of communities, along with the county fair and the circus, which usually came to Plattsburgh in the summer. The circus parade down Oak Street in Plattsburgh was a big part of circus day. Small children sat on front steps and watched the beautiful, spangled ladies on the horses or on the elephants, squealed at the clowns, and stared at the lions who glared balefully at onlookers from behind the bars of red and gold animal wagons. Later that afternoon or evening, people would go to the circus itself to watch the performers and animals bring magic, beauty and skill to the breathless audience underneath the big tent.

In Plattsburgh lovers of "moving pictures" could visit the Strand Theatre on Brinkerhoff Street to see their favorites of the silver screen.

A terrible fire in Au Sable Forks wiped out a large part of the business district in May 1925, leaving forty-five families homeless and one fireman dead. The alarm was given about one o'clock in the morning, but the fire had made great inroads before fire departments from Saranac Lake, Lake Placid, Plattsburgh, and Willsboro came to stop the conflagration. In the weeks that followed, people from all walks of life worked together to raise the village from the ashes and rebuild the community.

A fiery cross was burned near the Catholic cemetery on Prospect Street in Champlain in the mid-twenties. Newspaper accounts indicated that the Ku Klux Klan from

Plattsburgh Fire Station No. 1 was the scene of two contrasting types of fire prevention vehicles in 1925—horse-drawn and motorized. Courtesy of the Clinton County Historical Museum

Vermont was responsible, but this was never proved.

The Sheridan Ironworks in Champlain had experienced some changes in ownership and names, but it was the only business of its type continuously in operation for nearly a century.

A heat wave lasting three days in September 1929 took sixty thousand people in one day to the city beach to cool themselves off. The local board of health arranged transportation for children to the beach so that they, too, could escape the perilous heat.

Exuberance carried over into the economy. People were buying stocks in anticipation of making a fortune in a wildly fluctuating market. Many bought stocks on margin, and gambling on the market continued its upward spiral. But the stock market crashed in 1929 and the harsh impact affected the entire country. Local banks suffered, a few closing their doors. Local businessmen and other investors declared bankruptcy. The Great Depression had come and the ripple effect hurt everyone.

A Plattsburgh High School class in 1920 includes Gertrude Barker in the front row, center. Courtesy of the Clinton County Historical Museum

Three bathing beauties and their chaperone waited coyly for the photographer to do his stuff. Ladies' knees were being displayed for the very first time. Courtesy of Special Collections, Feinberg Library, SUNY, Plattsburgh

This posh houseboat was anchored in front of Hotel Champlain about 1920. The owners no doubt dined at the hotel. Courtesy of Special Collections, Feinberg Library, SUNY, Plattsburgh

Capt. Ell Rockwell, well-known steamboat captain, posed with Alan Booth on the steamboat Vermont. *Courtesy of the Clinton County Historical Museum*

The center of Peru was destroyed by fire on May 18, 1921. Inspecting the ruins next day, onlookers praised the Plattsburgh Fire Department which kept the blaze from consuming more of the town. Garden hoses and bucket brigades did what they could until help arrived. Fourteen buildings were destroyed. Courtesy of the Peru Free Library

From this power company came the electricity to light up Mooers. Courtesy of Special Collections, Feinberg Library, SUNY, Plattsburgh

One of the most important events on Margaret Street, Plattsburgh in 1921 was the laying of a cornerstone for the National Commercial Bank. Mr. John F. O'Brien, president, is about to insert a time capsule watched by other members of the board. John P. Benson, architect, is on O'Brien's right. Courtesy of the Clinton County Historical Museum

Chazy Marble Lime Company's kilns operated from 1925 to 1944. This new two-story building was built in 1923-24 and was made of stone from the old kiln. It held four upright steel kilns, a crusher, elevator, hydrator, screen, etc. It produced two hundred tons of limestone on a good day. Courtesy of the Clinton County Historical Museum

Ernest C. Gordon practiced law at 24 Clinton Street, Plattsburgh. Courtesy of Mary G. Leggett

The cars were tossed about like a giant's toy boxes during this collision on the Delaware and Hudson Railroad, October 1922. Courtesy of the Clinton County Historical Museum

The Standard Shoe House was located on Margaret Street. Under the rolled-up awning, the owners stand before their wares. Left to right are: Morton M. Markstone, S. Markstone, unidentified, and Abraham S. Markstone. Courtesy of Special Collections, Feinberg Library, SUNY, Plattsburgh

The Hotel Bridgeway stood beside the stone arch bridge in Keeseville. Courtesy of the Clinton County Historical Museum

Plattsburgh Ice Company manager George Lefebvre supervises gasoline-powered harvest in 1926. Courtesy of the Clinton County Historical Museum

Ice-fishing has long been a popular sport on Lake Champlain. The lake's bounty of smelt and perch were often featured on menus in the best restaurants in New York City. Men and vehicles have tested the ice for many years. Courtesy of the Clinton County Historical Museum

The 1925-26 Plattsburgh High School girls' basketball team posed with their coach, Clarence Kilburn. Courtesy of the Clinton County Historical Museum

This husky-looking sixth grade group from Broad Street School garnered 100 percent in a health contest in 1928. This probably signifies perfect attendance all year long. Courtesy of Special Collections, Feinberg Library, SUNY, Plattsburgh

In 1928 a monument commemorating the Battle of Valcour in 1776 was erected. Children of the American Revolution, Ruth Ladue and John Agnew of Plattsburgh, portrayed historical characters of the period. Courtesy of the Clinton County Historical Museum

A 1929 postcard depicts children playing by the Normal School Pond in Plattsburgh. Courtesy of Mary G. Leggett

Frank Duley waits on the platform of the Irona Creamery in Altona. Courtesy of Special Collections, Feinberg Library, SUNY, Plattsburgh

This small diner was located across from the Delaware and Hudson Railroad Station in Plattsburgh in 1929. In 1941-42 it was known as "Mazie's." The diner was later moved to Rooney Road north of Plattsburgh. Courtesy of the Clinton County Historical Museum

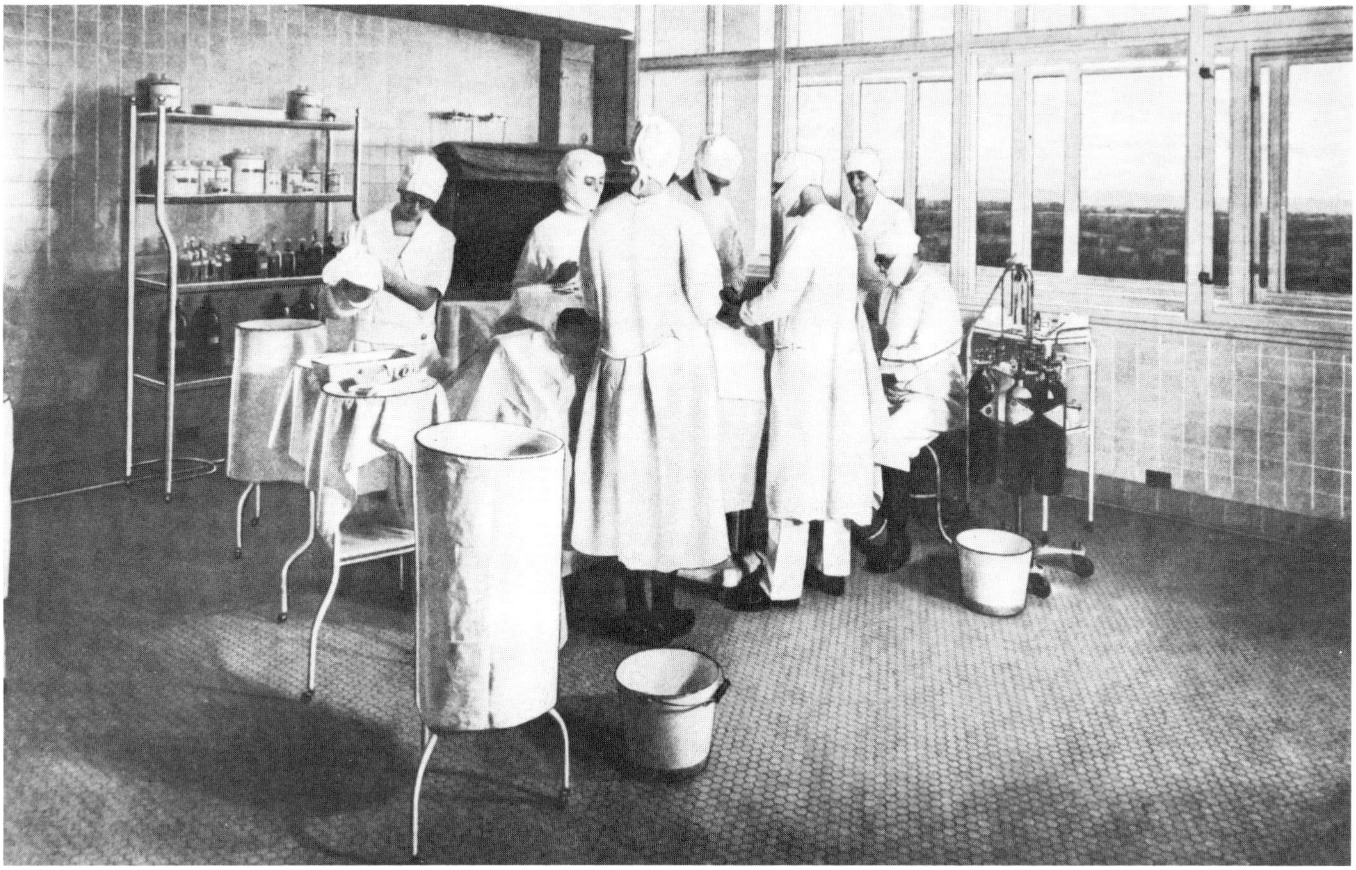

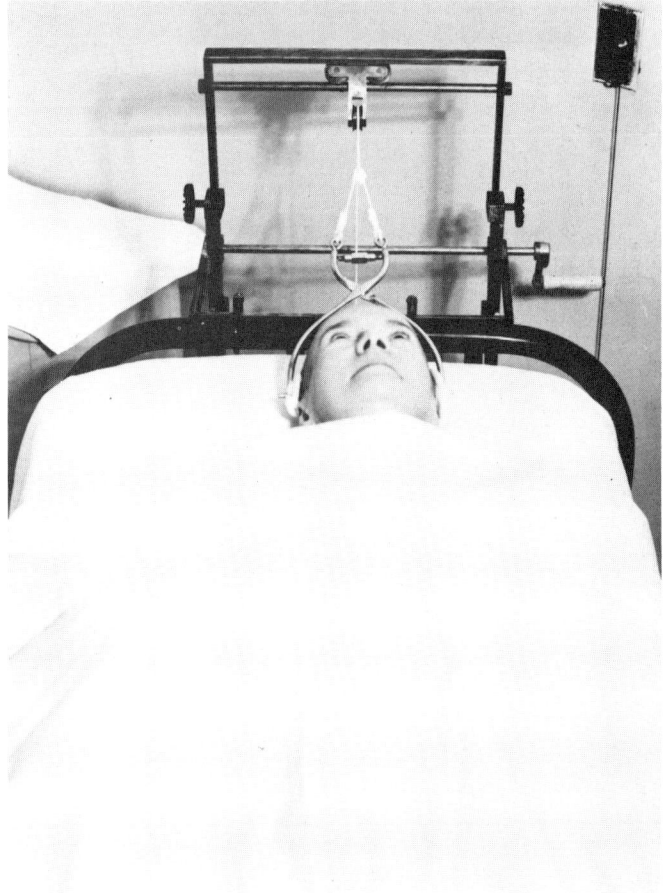

Surgeons and nurses work on a patient in one of the well-appointed operating rooms at the Physicians Hospital in Plattsburgh in 1929. The hospital was a beneficiary of the William H. Miner Foundation and was provided with the latest in both surgical and medical facilities. *Courtesy of Champlain Valley Physicians Hospital Medical Center*

The surgical forceps invented by Dr. Lyman Barton, Sr., were used for the first time in 1930 by Dr. Frank Ryan on a patient at the Champlain Valley Hospital. The patient was a Grey Nun who fell down the stairs and suffered a broken neck. The forceps helped hold the patient in place—and she recovered. *Courtesy of Special Collections, Feinberg Library, SUNY, Plattsburgh*

Summertime brought youngsters to the Normal School's pond to launch their toy boats on the pond's calm surface in 1934. Courtesy of Special Collections, Feinberg Library, SUNY, Plattsburgh

1930-1940

Hard times were here. The stock market crash affected industry and business alike, and the Great Depression hit Clinton County equally as hard as it did the rest of America. Men were out of work who had worked hard all their adult lives. Mills were forced to lay off men and to stagger work days so that all would be able to earn at least part of their pay.

When Franklin Delano Roosevelt was elected president in 1932, desperate people looked to him for help. His first step as president—a necessary one—stunned people, although they later understood the necessity of the bank holiday which closed banks for three days—March 6-9, 1933. However, payrolls were met on time. The new banking bill gave stability to those banks that had survived the debacle of 1929. The New Deal's next act was to set up the National Recovery Administration. Its goal was to encourage the nation's economic recovery and to combat unemployment. Trade codes that were designed to give work to millions of men and women went into effect. The forty-hour week became the rule, while unions, now legitimate, were allowed to bargain with employers.

The effect in Clinton County was extensive. Under Work Projects Administration men were set to work repairing and building roads, bridges and public buildings. Women made clothing, sheets, and comforters to be distributed to the needy. The Writer's Project, also under WPA, worked hard in Clinton County to write their section of New York State's history, which became a definitive work at that time and is still used in libraries today. WPA funds built Plattsburgh Public Library on Oak Street in 1939 and completed it in 1940.

A theme song during the initial exuberance of bringing in a new national administration was "Happy Days Are Here Again," as it was for recent Gov. Al Smith welcoming the repeal of Prohibition. But in Clinton County as the Depression went on, people listened and empathized with the melancholy song, "Brother Can You Spare a dime?" that was sweeping the nation via radio. And Plattsburgh now had a radio station, WMFF, owned and operated by Joel Scheier out of a few rooms in the Cumberland Hotel.

The Federal Surplus Commodities Corporation brought direct help to the needy in Clinton County. In the thirties each town had a town welfare officer who worked with County Welfare Commissioner Shirley Strack to determine who qualified for assistance. Trucks distributed surplus food every day among the fourteen towns in Clinton County. Apples, potatoes, butter, eggs, cheese—any food that was available in an excess amount—were distributed, along with clothing and bedding. Chits to buy groceries at the local stores in each town were also allocated.

Doctors, lawyers, other professionals, and business-

Plattsburgh Coach Line special bus took enthusiastic fans to the Roosevelt Ferry at Cumberland Head. Courtesy of the Clinton County Historical Museum

men were often paid by those they served in whatever goods the client could offer. Cord wood, garden produce, maple sugar and syrup, and plain hard work such as carpentry, painting, and other odd jobs served to pay the bills. It *was* a time when people worked together with a generosity of spirit that was typical of the Depression. Tramps came to Plattsburgh by "riding the rails." These were men down on their luck, looking for work wherever they could. It was a rare woman in Clinton County who did not dish up a square meal for any one of these men who knocked at her door, looking for work and only asking in return to be fed.

The federal government established the Civilian Conservation Corps in March 1933 under the direction of the Army, Labor Department, and the Forestry Service. The CCC, as it came to be known, promised employment and training for young men who were out of work. Some local men were shipped as far away as Idaho and Maine.

On January 5, 1935, Company 2207-V of the Civilian Conservation Corps was billeted at Plattsburgh municipal beach as part of the New Deal Program of 1933. Camp S-102, under Company Commander Donald L. Marsh and Camp Superintendent Carl B. Getman, was commissioned to take two hundred acres of swamp and sand dunes, including twenty-seven hundred feet of sand beach acquired through gifts and purchases, and turn it into one of the finest campsites in New York State. Roads were built, telephone lines were laid, a caretaker's house, a registration booth, water and sewage systems, and campsites for tents and trailers were all constructed by an outstanding group of men. Additional projects included reforestation, stream management, and foot paths on Lyon Mountain.

Despite the Depression, about thirty-four hundred automobile licenses were issued in January 1930. In that same year, the local chapter of the Women's Christian Temperance Union together with the Methodist, Presbyterian, Baptist, and Nazarene churches observed the tenth anniversary of Prohibition. Professor H. Otis Noyes from the Normal School was one of the principal speakers.

The *Plattsburgh Republican* published an announcement inviting women, when visiting downtown, to make use of their Women's Rest Room, located in the newspaper building at the corner of Marion and Clinton Street. They noted that the room was furnished with all conveniences including a telephone booth.

A headline in the 1930 *Daily Republican* announced the invention of television the previous year as the leading invention for that year.

In 1930 land previously obtained from Judge John Collins and added to by city funds was further augmented by the gift of more land bordering on the lake from Corydon Johnson of Plattsburgh. Thus did Plattsburgh acquire its city beach.

Plattsburgh's lack of public transportation was remedied when Leo Nash began a bus service in the early 1930s that approximated the trolley route. The bus line stayed in service for about twenty years until private automobiles made it unprofitable.

Movies at the Strand Theatre in Plattsburgh or in one of the small cinemas that dotted main streets in the villages of Clinton County cost a quarter. In winter, skating was highly popular. In Plattsburgh there was a skating rink behind the old high school opposite St. John's Church. That rink had a small warm-up hut and so did the rink at Mount Assumption Institute. Hardier souls skated on the Normal School pond and the pond in front of Physicians' Hospital, donning their skates while sitting in the snow. During the terrible winter of 1932-33 when the temperature fell to thirty-five below zero and the ice coated the roads, it was possible to skate all over town. There was also a very high man-made toboggan run behind the high school where one dragged a toboggan up the perilously slippery steps and whizzed down the run. The hill beside Lieutenant Governor Conway's house on Broad Street was filled with children on sleds while the more daring

Soldiers from the Military Barracks take their payroll from the Plattsburgh National Bank and Trust Company (later the National Commercial Bank and Trust Company, and now Key Bank, NA). Courtesy of Special Collections, Feinberg Library, SUNY, Plattsburgh

The largest peacetime maneuvers in the United States were held in and around Plattsburgh Barracks in 1939. Over fifty thousand troops participated. Courtesy of Special Collections, Feinberg Library, SUNY, Plattsburgh

youngsters took their Flexible Flyers down the hill on Boynton Avenue.

The A & P Grocery chain came to Plattsburgh, as did the Grand Union. Plattsburgh Business Institute on Oak Street was still turning out secretarial, accounting, and general business graduates. Ayerst, McKenna and Harrison Ltd., a Canadian pharmaceutical firm, opened a United States branch in Rouses Point, establishing a modest facility to manufacture its products.

And each summer the citizens' Military Training Camp came to Plattsburgh for exercises. So did the Reserve Officers' Training Camp with its full quota of young college men. Young ladies, properly chaperoned by matrons of the city, were introduced to members of ROTC at dances given at the Witherill Hotel. The final event of the season was the Scabbard and Blade dinner dance held at Hotel Champlain.

The largest peacetime war games were held in 1939, representing the biggest mobilization of troops in the U.S. since World War I. Over fifty-thousand troops from the First Army converged on Clinton County for the maneuvers during an extremely hot summer. Sixty-eight percent was National Guard, 30 percent Regular Army, and 2 percent organized reserves. Four guard divisions were from New York, New Jersey and New England. Troop convoys jammed the roads leading into Clinton County and the encampments were spread over Plattsburgh, Peru, and Schuyler Falls. Permits had to be secured for the property's use. The two weeklong maneuvers cost two million dollars, and cost the lives of seven men. The military learned that it needed more money and more training to prepare men for war.

Hawkins Hall was named for George Knight Hawkins, principal of Plattsburgh Normal School, who was the moving force in the new Normal School's design and construction after a fire destroyed the old school on January 29, 1929. Courtesy of the Clinton County Historical Museum

The interior of Sharron's Department Store in 1931 shows the jewelry counter and women's apparel. This fine department store was located on Margaret Street in Plattsburgh. Courtesy of the Clinton County Historical Museum

Merkel's Store on Margaret Street, Plattsburgh was photographed in 1930. It was flanked on one side by Gordon's Boot Shop and on the other by Jacques Drug Store, a popular hang-out for high school and college students who gathered at the soda fountain. Courtesy of Special Collections, Feinberg Library, SUNY, Plattsburgh

The Baptist Church on the corner of Oak and Court Street in Plattsburgh as it looked before its destruction by fire in 1931. Courtesy of Richard Ward

The Baptist Church burned down on January 2, 1931. Parishioners worshipped at the Temple Beth Israel Synagogue across Oak Street until a new church could be built. Courtesy of the Clinton County Historical Museum

A Dairymen's League railroad car waits on a railroad siding in Peru Village. Courtesy of the Clinton County Historical Museum

The flag flies in front of the U.S. Customs House in Mooers. This was all that stood between Canada and the United States—and relations have always been friendly. Courtesy of Special Collections, Feinberg Library, SUNY, Plattsburgh

The Plattsburgh Police Department in May 30, 1935 consisted of: (front row) John Frederick, Chief Clifford Fleming, and Elmer Gray; (second row) John Sweeney and Arthur "Mac" McCooey; (back row) Jim Russell, Ed Sweeney, Emmett Ducatte, Hank Dominy, Joseph McGuire, and Wilfred Trombley. Courtesy of the Clinton County Historical Museum

On June 4, 1938, Postmaster Arthur Sharron sent the following letter to Miss Julia Detraz at the Normal School:

Dear Miss Detraz:

I am sending you one of the pictures taken at the airport May 19 in which the children from your class appear quite prominently. I thought they would enjoy seeing the picture. It certainly came out better than we expected because it wasn't a very clear day.

It was very nice of you to bring the children down to help take part in the ceremony of our first air mail. We hope this will soon be an everyday occurrence, but at least the children can always say that they saw the first.

Courtesy of the Clinton County Historical Museum

In 1935 Capt. Lorenzo Hagglund raised the gunboat Philadelphia *from the bottom of the lake at the site of the Battle of Valcour. Hagglund toured both sides of the lake to display the vessel, then erected a shed for permanent display in Willsboro. His heirs conveyed the ship to the Smithsonian Institution in Washington, D.C., where it has been scientifically treated with preservatives and is on permanent display. It is considered a rare example of an eighteenth century warship in a fine state of preservation. Courtesy of the Clinton County Historical Museum*

At the raising of the gunboat Philadelphia, *three eighteenth-century cannons were recovered. This operation was carried out by Lorenzo Hagglund in 1935 at the site of the Battle of Valcour. Boat and cannon are now in the custody of the Smithsonian Institution in Washington, D.C. Courtesy of the Clinton County Historical Museum*

The Chazy Fire Department truck is ready for any emergency call in 1937, even to the brooms in the back of the truck. Courtesy of the Clinton County Historical Museum

Fort Montgomery, at Rouses Point, was partially demolished to provide stone for construction of the Rouses Point bridge which opened in 1937. Courtesy of the Clinton County Historical Museum

Jack Dempsey, the famous world boxing champion, visited Nash's Bowling Alley, Plattsburgh, in the late 1930s. Courtesy of Jean McCooey Carey

Brother George and Brother Lawrence posed with the Mount Assumption Institute 1937-38 basketball team. The team members were (left to right): Miller, Chauvin, Dumois, Barrett, LaPlante, Hicks, Fountain, Cavanaugh, Turcotte, and Navarro. Courtesy of the Clinton County Historical Museum

It looks like recess time at the old Peru High School, probably in the late twenties or early thirties. The new Peru High School was built in 1939 and its first senior class graduated that year. Courtesy of Special Collections, Feinberg Library, SUNY, Plattsburgh

Clark Street in Dannemora is overshadowed by the prison wall, built between 1884 and 1887. Two types of horse power are shown in this 1940 photograph. Courtesy of the Clinton County Historical Museum

Mayor Leander Bouyea welcomes the Eightieth Regiment to Plattsburgh on September 26, 1941. The food was warm and the welcome was hearty from the citizens of Plattsburgh gathered at the Macdonough Monument. Courtesy of the Clinton County Historical Museum

Chapter 11

1940-1945

The war in Europe was escalating and the threat of armed conflict involving Americans was imminent. On December 7, 1941, the Japanese attacked Pearl Harbor. President Roosevelt announced to the nation that the United States had declared war. One person recalling that day said the Army Engineers, returning from training off the coast of North Carolina, were marching up Peru Street back to the Barracks at the same time the attack on Pearl Harbor was announced.

Clinton County men volunteered readily for World War II, a war fought on two fronts—in Europe and the Pacific. Although a draft board was set up, Clinton County sent its share of volunteers, many of whom were killed and others seriously wounded. In some way, the war touched everyone in Clinton County—either a son, a relative, a neighbor, or a friend had gone to the front. Rationing food and gas occurred almost immediately, and women entered the work force in droves to replace men who had gone to war.

The Berst-Forster-Dixfield Company, one of the area's major employers, began to hire more women. Pal Blade, Imperial and other industries in the county did likewise, so Clinton County had its own versions of "Rosie the Riveter."

People received censored letters from overseas and they spoke in hushed tones about loved ones in the war. Posters admonished, "Loose lips sink ships."

Everyone participated in the war effort. They saved tin cans, first carefully squashed flat, and newspapers. Children saved their allowances to buy savings stamps, pasted in a small book to put toward a War Bond.

War Bond rallies encouraged people to save their money to buy bonds for Uncle Sam. Victory gardens sprang up everywhere and butter was scarce. In place of butter, oleomargarine came in a large white pound brick with the coloring agent enclosed. It was the job of the busy housewife, or children impressed into duty, to combine the color with the oleomargarine to produce a pound of uniform yellow color. That *never* happened. It was always streaked unevenly despite the mauling it received—so that "buttering" the bread became an adventure.

Pathé News at local cinemas brought the war home visually for the first time—and it was frightening. Air raid wardens patrolled every block to make sure that blackout shades were pulled down and curtains secured, so that no light could appear to guide the enemy. The sound of the fire alarm was the signal for an air raid drill. During school drills children crouched under their desks for protection in case of attack.

Both men and women were airplane spotters. From the Physicians' Hospital roof and other elevated places in the county, they scanned the skies, identifying any airplane that flew overhead, ready to give the alarm if necessary. Even children learned to pick out the different airplanes.

Sunday drives ceased, to conserve gas. Block dances were a common form of entertainment.

The details of everyday life became submerged in the drama being played on a world stage. But life went on in Clinton County, despite rationing, shortages and the ever-present worry over the men and women (nurses, WACS, and WAVES) who were on active duty.

The Berst-Forster-Dixfield Company, celebrating its twenty-fifth anniversary, changed its name to BFD. And the airfield that had been located next to the factory on North Margaret Street near today's Georgia-Pacific was gone. The Clinton County Airport was built in 1942-43 on Route 3 west of Plattsburgh. BFD began negotiations with the county so that its planes could land at the new airport, but its own airfield was still in use.

In 1945 World War II ended. Who could know that a very different world was about to take shape?

This is a float for the Fourth of July parade in 1942 from the Berst-Forster-Dixfield plant in Plattsburgh. Workers on the float represent the union. Courtesy of the Clinton County Historical Museum

Now a bustling marina on Lake Champlain at Plattsburgh, Dock & Coal Company Inc., offered a different type of service in the 1940s. Courtesy of Special Collections, Feinberg Library, SUNY, Plattsburgh

An armored car at the Barracks during World War I was no doubt impressive in its day, but it looks quaint by modern standards. Courtesy of Special Collections, Feinberg Library, SUNY, Plattsburgh

During World War II the U.S. government gave an aircraft sheet metal training course at Georgia-Pacific in what was originally the Lozier Boat shop. This picture shows a gathering of men promoting the project. Included are the heads of the teachers' training college and the Plattsburgh city schools. Courtesy of Special Collections, Feinberg Library, SUNY, Plattsburgh

A patriotic World War II pageant took place in the Plattsburgh High School auditorium. Courtesy of the Clinton County Historical Museum

Young ladies from Plattsburgh Teachers' College headed for the apple orchards to pick the crop in 1944. Courtesy of Special Collections, Feinberg, Library, SUNY, Plattsburgh

Section VI: The Promise of the Future

Plattsburgh Air Base Operations Control Tower was the first to be painted "Adirondack Brown," the new tan and brown exterior. Many more buildings have received the new look, some under contract, but many of the one-story, easy-to-paint variety were done by volunteers. A total of 292 people were involved in the effort, known as Operation Facelift. Courtesy of the Plattsburgh Press-Republican

1945-1988

The end of World War II in 1945 signaled the return of servicemen and women to their homes in Clinton County. At the Barracks, the Navy's temporary use of the facility (known as Camp Macdonough) gave way to an Army Air Force convalescent hospital. Once again declared surplus by the Army in 1946, the property was acquired by the state of New York which established Champlain College there. The college was one of three institutions known collectively as the Upper New York Associated Colleges for war veterans. Under the G.I. Bill, veterans were financially assisted in acquiring a higher education. In 1949, when 1,787 students were enrolled at the college, total fees were $614. Student housing cost $15 per month and married student housing was $29 per month. Champlain College was not destined for a long life, however.

In the early 1950s the Air Force, now an independent service, was attracted to the Plattsburgh area in its search for a suitable site for a strategic air command base. The prospect of the Air Force taking over the home of Champlain College did not have the citizenry's unanimous approval. Many opposed it on the grounds that a more appropriate location for a huge air base could be found elsewhere in the county, further removed from Plattsburgh's urban center. But the opposite view prevailed and Champlain College closed its doors to make way for Plattsburgh Air Force Base.

During the 1950s a runway and other facilities were built. Housing named after Senator Homer Capehart was constructed for base personnel and their families. Soon a "new base" existed in addition to the "old base" on the original Barracks site. The 380th Bombardment Wing arrived in 1955 and has remained operational at Plattsburgh since that time. Clinton County residents have become familiar with the sight of B-47s, B-52s, FB-111s, KC-97 and KC-135 tankers in the North Country skies.

In 1988 a total of approximately 3,700 Air Force personnel and dependents are county residents.

Clinton County made front page news in the *New York Herald Tribune* on September 8, 1960. " 'Digging Through Hell' for 12 I.C.B.M. sites" ran the headline. The story covered construction workers' efforts to penetrate rock for the excavation of 174-feet-deep holes which would serve as silos for Atlas intercontinental ballistic missiles bearing nuclear warheads. Each hole measured fifty-two feet in diameter and was connected through a one hundred-foot tunnel to a control center. An estimated eight thousand cubic yards of concrete were poured per site.

The silos were scattered around the county at Champlain, Mooers, Ellenburg, Harrigan Corners, Chazy Lake, Clayburg, Sugarbush, and Ausable Chasm. Two of the sites were located in Essex County at Boquet and Willsboro, and two in Vermont at Alburg and Swanton.

This B-47 stands at the entrance to the new section of the Plattsburgh Air Force Base, welcoming visitors. At Christmas a huge Santa Claus sits on top of the airplane as PAFB joins with its neighbors to celebrate the holidays. Courtesy of the Clinton County Historical Museum

In a change of command of the 380th Bombardment Wing at the Plattsburgh Air Base, Col. C. Jerome Jones, second from right, turns over the office to Col. Richard N. Goddard, right. Two visiting generals attended the 1987 ceremony. Courtesy of the Plattsburgh Press-Republican

The *Tribune* reported that a new squadron of perhaps five hundred men would be assigned to Plattsburgh Air Force Base to staff the missile installations. As the Cuban crisis developed in 1962, the missiles were put into operational readiness. But by June 25, 1965, the eighty-two-foot high Atlas liquid fuel missile had become operationally obsolete.

Another crucial element in the county's economy is its institutions of higher learning. In addition to its arts and science program, State University College at Plattsburgh offers professional programs in nursing, education, speech and hearing, and human services. A school of business and economics has been recently established in 1985. Throughout the tenure of Gov. Nelson A. Rockefeller, a major expansion of the campus took place. Twenty-two new buildings were completed between 1963 and 1978, including those designed for the fine and performing arts; science; library; physical education; institutional support services; residences and dining halls. The current enrollment in 1988 is approximately fifty-eight hundred students with eight hundred faculty and staff members.

The peaceful demeanor of SUNY Plattsburgh today belies the tumult that took place on campus in 1970, in

Laura Jean Ingalls, assistant librarian at the Plattsburgh Public Library, and Mayor John Tyrell (right) accept a book about the Atlas missile from an executive of the General Dynamics Corporation. Courtesy of the Clinton County Historical Museum

Gov. Nelson A. Rockefeller, in hard hat, operates the pile-driver at the groundbreaking ceremony for the first Feinberg Library at State University College, Plattsburgh in 1959. The edifice is now known as the Redcay Building, housing faculty offices. Courtesy of Special Collections, Feinberg Library, SUNY, Plattsburgh

common with other universities across the United States, when students protested American involvement in Vietnam. A plaque in front of the Kehoe Administration Building recalls six student deaths at Kent State University and subsequent demonstrations on the Plattsburgh campus.

Clinton County boasts another institution of higher learning at Clinton Community College which occupies the former Hotel Champlain at Bluff Point. After an interlude of use by the Society of Jesus in the 1950s and 1960s, when it was known as Bellarmine College, the imposing structure was purchased by the Clinton County Legislature. The community college opened its doors in 1969 and now has a current enrollment of 1,600 students taught by nearly one hundred faculty members.

After renovating the interior of the building, the college has committed itself to construction of a health, physical education, convocation, and arts center. An unsurpassed view of Lake Champlain, the same vista enjoyed by Presidents McKinley and Taft, is one of the college's unique physical features.

Route 9 north from Plattsburgh to Champlain via the village of Chazy served travelers for many years as the road to the Canadian border and thence to Montreal and the province of Quebec. In 1967, coinciding with Expo '67, the unforgettable World's Fair in Montreal, a dramatic change occurred in travel to the border and beyond. Interstate 87, or the Northway, was completed, reducing travel between Albany, the state capital, and Plattsburgh to three hours. Although subsequently removed, telephones were installed on the highway through the lonely, uninhabited stretches of the Adirondacks. Never to be entirely eliminated, the North Country's sense of isolation was significantly reduced by the advent of this superhighway.

Plattsburgh's future was significantly altered by the Northway, also. Between the city and I-87 on its western boundary, shopping centers and businesses began to spring up. During the next two decades Upper Cornelia Street or Route 3, the western artery, was fully developed, culminating with the opening of the Champlain Centre North in 1987.

The tourist industry, always an important factor in Clinton County's economic well-being, grew rapidly. Today there are no fewer than forty-five motels and bed and breakfast sites offering accommodation to travelers. In winter a multiplicity of shopping centers attracts Canadian and local shoppers; in summer, the city beach and state parks at Point Au Roche, Plattsburgh and Au Sable Point lure thousands of Canadians to the cool, clear

Little space remained on the Plattsburgh Municipal Beach when the sun shone brightly on June 30, 1963. This photograph belies the size of Lake Champlain— more than one hundred miles long and ten miles wide. Courtesy of Special Collections, Feinberg Library, SUNY, Plattsburgh

waters of Lake Champlain.

Downtown Plattsburgh is the place to be on the second Saturday in July when the Mayor's Cup is held in Cumberland Bay. The sailing regatta attracts large numbers of boats of all sizes which can be watched from vantage points on the shore or from the top of the Macdonough Monument. The Historical Association provides a double attraction by staging its annual outdoor flea market in Trinity Park. Thousands of local people and visitors attend these colorful events.

Year-round ferry service from Cumberland Head to Grand Isle, Vermont, initiated by the Lake Champlain Transportation Company during the winter of 1976-77, allows travelers to cross the lake's icy expanse quickly. The company's other ferries operate seasonally. A joint New York-Vermont venture resulted in construction of a new bridge at Rouses Point, dedicated in 1987.

A huge increase in the number of recreational boats on Lake Champlain indicates to local residents that their lake is no longer the undiscovered waterway they imagined. The popularity of sailing and power boats has multiplied the number of marinas on both sides of the lake, giving summer pleasure to thousands but causing concern to environmentalists. New York State's purchase of Valcour and Crab islands has placed the future of these islands in the public domain. In 1987 the Clinton County Historical Association acquired a conservation easement for the Valcour Island Lighthouse, built in 1871. The society now has the right to preserve the beacon as a monument to the historical importance of maritime traffic on the lake.

Music, art and drama have always been important to Clinton County's residents. During the 1950s the Community Concert Association brought professional performers to Plattsburgh in an annual subscription series. By 1962 the Council on the Arts had evolved, beginning a quarter century of excellence in presentation of the performing arts. Young adults today remember their first

The Korean Veterans Memorial Bridge connecting Rouses Point with the Alburg Peninsula in Vermont was opened in September 1987. It will be toll-free and will replace the old swing-span bridge which it parallels and which is being dismantled.

Including approaches, the new bridge is about 7,500 feet long and provides a fifty-five-foot vertical clearance of the water. It was dedicated on September 22, 1987, by Vermont's Gov. Madeleine Kunin and New York's Lt. Gov. Stanley Lundine. Courtesy of the Plattsburgh Press-Republican

Officers and workers for the Community Concert Association held banquets such as this one at the Cumberland Hotel in the 1950s. Paul H. Hartman of the college English faculty is to be seen at the head of the table. Elva Sartwell of Peru and Jay Davern, lawyer of Plattsburgh, are among the music enthusiasts. Courtesy of the Clinton County Historical Museum

---

exposure to professional musical groups when the Arts Council's children's committee started to take a variety of musical programs to the schools.

The College-Community Orchestra gave amateur musicians a chance to study and perform serious orchestral music. Today the county is blessed with orchestral and choral societies and an astonishing number of smaller performing groups. Clinton County has much more than its fair share of talent in the visual arts, both in the community and on the State University campus. The Little Theatre group originated in Clinton County in the 1930s and continues to present plays on a regular basis.

An Imagination Celebration, organized by the Council on the Arts for Clinton County, has become a dazzling community event attended by many parents and children. In this 1987 photograph a performer entertains children in the Plattsburgh Public Library. Courtesy of the Council on the Arts for Clinton County

Priceless collections of historical artifacts are housed in three museums. The County Museum in City Hall, Plattsburgh, administered by the Historical Association, interprets local history through its fine collections. The Kent-Delord House Museum, a historic house, has witnessed nearly two hundred years of colorful North County history and still welcomes visitors into its gracious rooms. The Alice T. Miner Colonial Collection in Chazy contains a fascinating array of decorative arts objects collected by Mrs. William H. Miner and displayed in a stately mansion on the village's main street.

In 1954 the Clinton-Essex Library System was formed to provide library service throughout the two counties. (Franklin County was added in 1962.) The bookmobile began its weekly schedule of delivering books to rural areas in 1955, offering country dwellers a wide selection of books and records.

Until the founding of the Champlain Valley Hospital by the Order of the Grey Nuns soon after the turn of the century, Clinton County had no hospital facilities. Doctors such as Cassius Silver, David Kellogg, and Joseph La Rocque operated on their patients on kitchen tables while sterilizing their instruments with water kept boiling on the stove.

When the Grey Nuns approached local residents and businessmen to help underwrite a hospital, they began a tradition of community involvement which culminated in the construction of the present Champlain Valley Physicians Hospital Medical Center.

Champlain Valley Hospital opened its doors in 1910. The following year, Physicians' Hospital came into being at 116 Court Street, also in Plattsburgh. Soon the need for a larger building became critical. Dr. Silver's friendship with Mr. and Mrs. William H. Miner led to Mr. Miner's decision to donate a hospital to the community. In 1926 the grand new medical facility opened at 100 Beekman Street on a site chosen by Mrs. Miner.

The two hospitals continued to operate independently until the early 1960s. But by that time neither unit conformed to modern regulatory standards. Duplication of services and the difficulty in attracting medical specialists to the North Country were other factors in the 1967 decision to merge the hospitals. Champlain Valley Hospital, adjacent to the college, was sold to the state of New York for expansion of its campus.

A local fundraising campaign netting $1.4 million was the nucleus of funds required to build a new facility attached to the existing Physicians Hospital. On May 15, 1972, patients were transferred from the old CV Hospital and a new era of health care began at the Champlain Valley Physicians Hospital Medical Center. In 1926 Physicians' Hospital was a 212-bed facility; in 1987 the Medical Center admitted 12,286 patients.

Clinton County is entering its third century on a wave of prosperity and optimism. If our hardy forebears could visit us now, surely they would think that their faith in this northern land was justified.

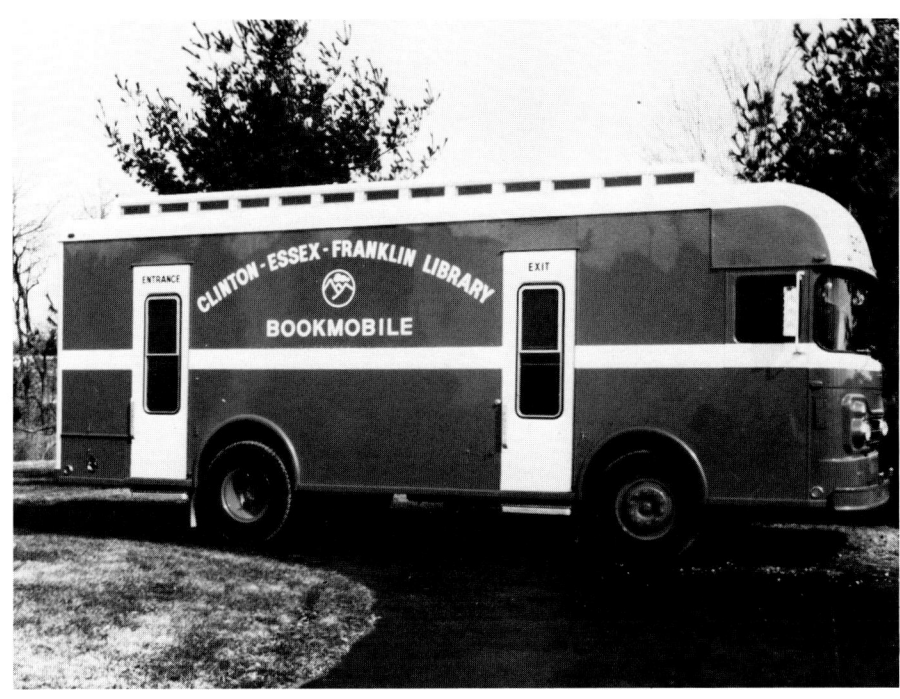

A welcome sight in Clinton County is the big red bookmobile from the Clinton–Essex–Franklin Library System. Rural residents in the small hamlets and settlements look forward to browsing among the three thousand books that are housed on the bookmobile. Starting in 1954 this service is still going strong today. Courtesy of the Clinton-Essex-Franklin Library System

Clinton County Dairymen's Cooperative Creamery was located off Boynton Avenue across Weed Street about 1948-50. Courtesy of Special Collections, Feinberg Library, SUNY, Plattsburgh

A luncheon for Thomas E. Dewey took place at the Hotel Witherill on September 25, 1950. On his left is Assemblyman James A. Fitzpatrick. Other prominent citizens gathered for a chat after lunch. Courtesy of Special Collections, Feinberg Library, SUNY, Plattsburgh

Seen in this 1950s photograph with his daughter-in-law, Hulda Bredenberg McLellan, Hugh McLellan was nearing the end of his life. An architect with roots in the North Country, Hugh McLellan was commissioned to design the Samuel de Champlain monument on Cumberland Avenue in Plattsburgh. With his son, Charles Woodberry (Woody) McLellan and Hulda, Hugh compiled the cemetery records of Clinton County which are so helpful to genealogists. Courtesy of Special Collections, Feinberg Library, SUNY, Plattsburgh

A formal gathering of Elks took place at the Plattsburgh Lodge on Cumberland Avenue. Edward J. Lapham was the Grand Exalted Ruler from 1953 to 1954. Courtesy of the Clinton County Historical Museum

Senator Ronald B. Stafford smiles for the camera as Gov. Nelson A. Rockefeller shakes Sidney Spiegel's hand. The fourth man is unidentified. Courtesy of Special Collections, Feinberg Library, SUNY, Plattsburgh

Obviously Saturday was shopping day in downtown Plattsburgh in the 1950s. Courtesy of the Clinton County Historical Museum

This aerial view of downtown Plattsburgh in the late 1950s shows the National Commercial Bank (later Key Bank) in the center of the photograph. Courtesy of Key Bank N.A.

In the 1960s, the Clinton Correctional Facility staff attended classes on the various aspects of working with the inmates. Courtesy of Special Collections, Feinberg Library, SUNY, Plattsburgh

Attorneys Jay Davern, Orville Dunn, and Harold Jerry received awards at a Clinton County Bar Association meeting on August 22, 1964. All three men were recognized for a half-century of service as attorneys and counselors. Courtesy of the Clinton County Historical Museum

Former Assemblyman James A. Fitzpatrick, standing at the microphone, and a crowd of well-wishers welcomed Henry Cabot Lodge (foreground) to Plattsburgh during his vice-presidential bid. Courtesy of Harold Hart

In 1968 three teenagers, scuba-diving in Lake Champlain just off Cliff Haven, found two brass cannons which had been cast overboard from the Muskellunge in 1759. One of the cannons is on long-term loan to the Clinton County Historical Museum from the state of New York. Courtesy of the Clinton County Historical Museum and Frank Pabst

Flames leap into the air, eerily illuminating the windows at Prescott's factory in Keeseville. The building was put up for auction in 1967; this picture was taken in May 1969. Courtesy of the Clinton County Historical Museum

Service clubs, such as the Lions Club, Kiwanis and Rotary, play a large role in maintaining a high quality of life for Clinton County citizens. In this picture "Mr. Lion," Jerry LaBombard, visits the playground where he and his fellow Lions Club members put together equipment for the intermediate school children. Students raised half the money for the new equipment; the school district paid the other half. About twenty members of the Peru Lions Club gave their time to put together and install the playground equipment. Courtesy of the Plattsburgh Press-Republican

An interior photograph of the Union Hotel bar located at 17 Margaret Street, Plattsburgh. It was a popular spot for both Champlain College and Plattsburgh State students. Courtesy of the Clinton County Historical Museum

Crescent saws were used in ice harvesting in the 1920s. This one is held by Bill Haron in 1986. Courtesy of the Clinton County Historical Museum

A new county fire control system was installed in the city station on Cornelia Street. It carries the name of Clinton County Communications Center. Computer-based, it allows for efficient monitoring of fires anywhere in the county. Randy Marshall is shown above at the new console, where two dispatchers can work independently or in concert. Courtesy of the Plattsburgh Press-Republican

CART, the county-wide transportation system, was started in 1983, and in 1987 it was extended to street coverage in Plattsburgh. The picture shows Pamela Delamater, Clinton County planning assistant, and George Merrill of Bridgewater Transport, which has operated the service since June 1987. Courtesy of the Plattsburgh Press-Republican

The Plattsburgh Cardinals emerged as the 1986-87 NCAA Division III champions in hockey. They ended the season with a 33 to 6 record after defeating the runner-up team of Oswego at the Plattsburgh State Field House. Courtesy of State University College at Plattsburgh

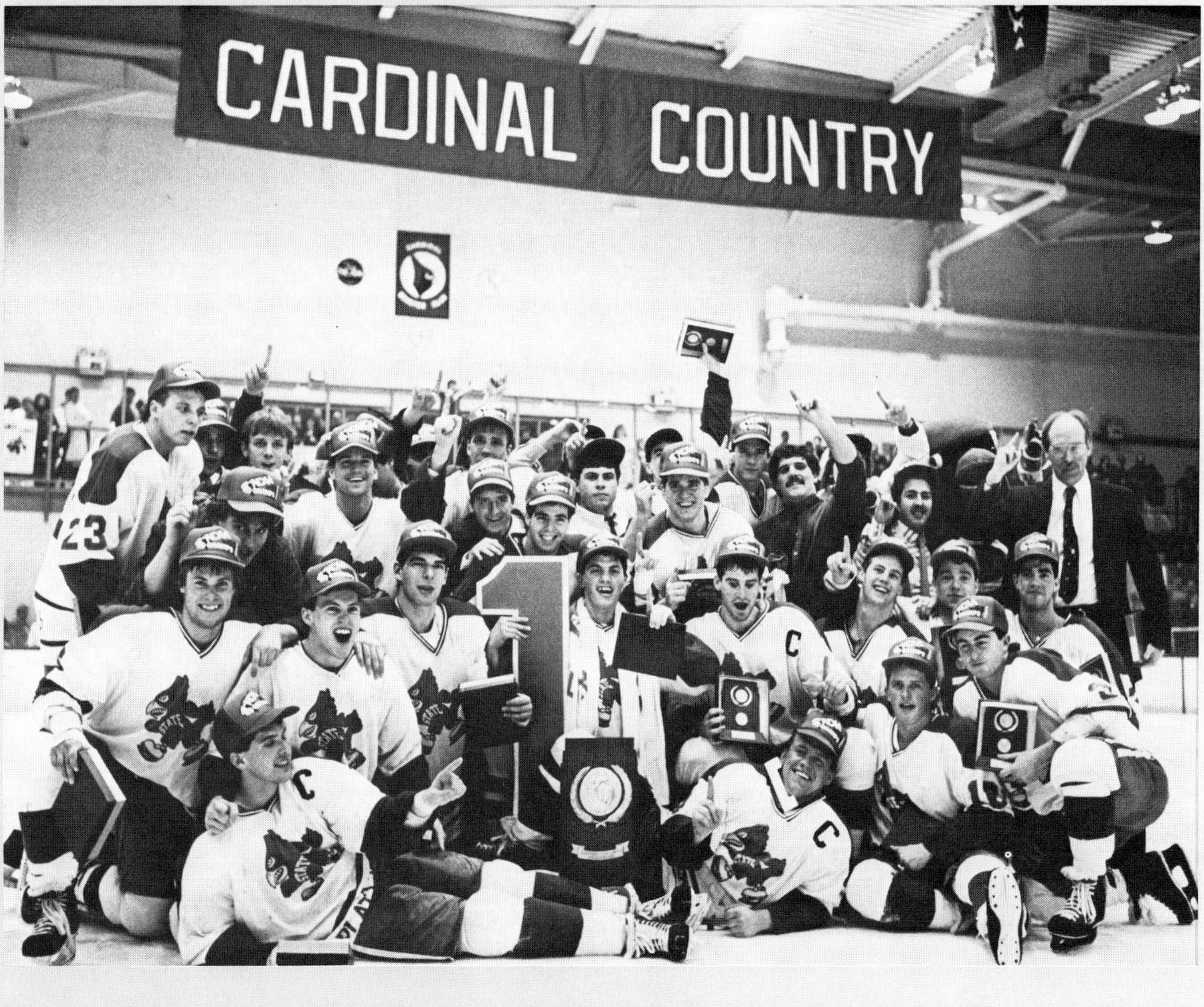

Today, only ruins are visible from the I-87 bridge over the Saranac River between exits 36 and 37. The factory that once stood there originally housed the Fredenberg Falls Pulp Company, incorporated in 1894. Later it was occupied by the American Carbide Works. The river has always been important to industry in Clinton County. In the nineteenth century nearly one hundred mills were located along its banks. Courtesy of Special Collections, Feinberg Library, SUNY, Plattsburgh

A plane's view of the Clinton County Airport in Plattsburgh was made in 1987. In recent years the two main runways were resurfaced, and new lighting and navigational systems installed. Courtesy of the Plattsburgh Press-Republican

Ground was broken in November 1987 for a new Clinton County jail. It is to be erected on the site of the old Super 87 Drive-in Theatre, near exit 38 of the Northway. The construction contractor, Murnane Associates, will own the building and the county will lease it. Courtesy of the Plattsburgh Press-Republican

The Chazy and Westport Telephone service underwent important improvements in 1987. The building in Chazy, shown here, received both interior and exterior changes. The technology has been improved by computerizing operations, better switching stations and more efficient service to sparsely populated areas. Courtesy of the Plattsburgh Press-Republican

Two Plattsburgh High School students won the top spots in the 1988 Youth Concerto Contest. Shown is Julie Lee, 14, top winner, practicing a Schumann piano concerto with the Champlain Valley Symphony. The orchestra, together with the Division of Youth, sponsored the contest. At the January concert, the runner-up Daniel Kimmage, 18, performed part of the Rachmaninov piano concerto Number 2. Courtesy of the Plattsburgh Press-Republican

Verdantique Park, a long-discussed plan to improve the banks of the Saranac River, will move into the construction stage early in 1988. This is made possible by a state grant from the Environmental Quality Bond funds. The project envisages hiking and bicycle paths from the mouth of the river to the western city limits, to be completed over several years, as money becomes available. The present plan calls for a fish ladder at the Imperial Mill dam to further the development of the salmon fishery on the river. Courtesy of the Plattsburgh Press-Republican

The Clinton County Legislature in 1987 consisted of, back row, left to right, Richard S. Perry, Robert M. Garrow, William H. LePage, Roy J. McGee, and Lawrence Paquette; front row, left to right, Donald L. Garrant, Howard S. Tedford, Susan R. Castine, Melvin R. Bruno, and Samuel J. Trombley.

The Clinton County Legislature in 1988 consisted of, back row, left to right, Richard S. Perry, Donald L. Garrant, William H. LePage, Lawrence Paquette, and Gregory B. Campbell; front row, left to right, Candis M. Luck, Howard S. Tedford, Susan R. Castine, Melvin R. Bruno, and Samuel J. Trombley.

BIBLIOGRAPHY

Baker, Sarah. *The Saranac Valley.* 2 vols. Saranac, N.Y., 1970.

Barcomb, Peg, comp. *Rouses Point: Centennial Year 1877, 1977.* Printed 1977.

Barnett, Lincoln. *The Ancient Adirondacks.* New York: Time-Life Books, 1974.

Beekmantown Bicentennial Committee. *Beekmantown, A Landmark in a Passageway.* Addie L. Shields, ed. 1976.

Bicentennial Committee of Mooers, N.Y. *Historical review of town of Mooers.* Elizabethtown, N.Y.: Denton Publications, 1976.

Bicentennial Committee of Peru, N.Y. *History of Peru, New York.* Keeseville, N.Y.: Adirondack Litho, 1976.

Clinton County Historical Museum. *Clinton Prison at Dannemora.* Plattsburgh, 1987.

Clinton County Historical Museum. "The Iron Industry in Clinton County." Plattsburgh: printed sheets.

Conners, Frank P. *Altona in Retrospect.* No date or publisher.

Crockett, Walter Hill. *Vermont, the Green Mountain State.* 4 vols. New York: The Century History, 1921.

Curtis, Newton Martin. *From Bull Run to Chancellorsville.* New York: G. P. Putnam's Sons, 1906.

DeSormo, Maitland C. *The Heydays of the Adirondacks.* Saranac Lake: Adirondack Yesteryears, 1974.

Ellis, David M. et al. *A History of New York State.* Ithaca: Cornell University Press, 1967.

Everest, Allan S. *Briefly told, Plattsburgh, New York, 1784-1984.* Plattsburgh: Clinton County Historical Association, 1984.

Everest, Allan S. *Moses Hazen and the Canadian Refugees in the American Revolution.* Syracuse: Syracuse University Press, 1976.

Everest, Allan S. *Rum Across the Border.* Syracuse: Syracuse University Press, 1978.

Everest, Allan S. *The War of 1812 in the Champlain Valley.* Syracuse: Syracuse University Press, 1981.

French, J. H. *Gazetteer of the State of New York.* Syracuse: R. P. Smith, 1860.

Hill, Ralph Nading. *Lake Champlain, Key to Liberty.* Taftsville, Vt.: The Countryman Press, 1977.

Hurd, Duane H. *History of Clinton and Franklin Counties, New York.* Philadelphia: J. W. Lewis, 1880.

Kellogg, David S. *A Doctor at All Hours: The Private Journal of a Small-Town Doctor's Varied Life, 1886-1909.* Allan S. Everest, ed. Brattleboro, Vt.: Stephen Greene Press, 1970.

Mill Whistle, The. Newsletter of the BFD Company.

National Railway Historical Society, Connecticut Valley Chapter. *The Plattsburgh Traction Company, Plattsburgh, New York, 1895-1929.* 1971.

New York Lake Champlain Tercentenary Commission. *The Champlain Tercentenary.* Albany: J. B. Lyon Company, 1913.

New York State Commission. *Official Program of the Plattsburgh Centennial Celebration.* Albany: J. B. Lyon Company, 1914.

Nolan, Margaret, comp. and ed. *Yesterday, Today, Tomorrow—Black Brook—Au Sable Forks.* Elizabethtown: N.Y. Denton Publications, 1977.

North Country Notes. Monthly publication of the Clinton County Historical Association, Plattsburgh.

Plattsburgh Centenary Commission. *Dedication of the Thomas Macdonough Memorial.* Albany: J. B. Lyon Company, 1926.

Plattsburgh Daily Press. Souvenir Industrial Edition of Plattsburgh, 1897. Plattsburgh: W. Lansing & Son, 1897. Reprint by Corner-stone Bookshop, Plattsburgh, 1978.

Plattsburgh Public Library Local History Pamphlet File.

Shaughnessy, Jim. *The Delaware and Hudson.* Berkeley, California: Howell-North Books, 1967.

Sullivan, Nell J. B. and David K. Martin. *A History of the Town of Chazy, Clinton County, New York.* Burlington, Vt.: George Little Press, 1970.

The Antiquarian. Annual publication of the Clinton County Historical Association.

Town of Plattsburgh, N.Y. *Historical Sketches of the Town of Plattsburgh.* Elizabethtown, N.Y.: Denton Publications, 1975.

Watson, Winslow C. *The Military and Civil History of the County of Essex, New York.* Albany: J. Munsell, 1869.

White, Philip L. *Beekmantown, New York.* Austin: University of Texas Press, 1979.

York State Tradition. Various issues of this historical quarterly.

INDEX

A
Adirondacks, 11, 51, 201
agriculture, 32, 47, 49, 113
Air Force, 199
Albany, 12, 17, 32, 40, 51-53, 201
Alburg, Vt., 199
Alger, Sec. of War Russell A., 89
Altona, 20, 47, 51-52
American Revolution, 12, 14, 17, 31
Angellville, 20
architecture, 20, 22, 52
Arthur, Dr. Asa, 67
Arnold, Benedict, 14
Arnold, Elisha & Mary, 33
Arnold Hill, 20, 33, 49, 51, 67
Asbury, Bishop Francis, 22
Astor, John Jacob, 65
Auburn prison, 35
Au Sable, town of, 12, 17, 20, 22
Ausable Chasm, 199
Au Sable Forks, 20, 49, 67, 97, 115, 141, 167
Au Sable Point, 201
Au Sable R., 20, 49, 52
Averill, C. W., 35

B
Baker, E. C., 51
Baker Brothers, 67
Barton, Dr. Lyman, 138
Barton, Dr. Lyman Guy, 138, 140
Barton, Dr. Lyman Guy, Jr., 140
Barton, Dr. Philip, 140
Beekman, Dr. William, 14, 17
Beekmantown, 17, 20, 40, 47, 79-80, 113
Bellarmine College, 201
Belmont, 67
Birmingham Falls, 49
Black Brook, 17, 20, 49
Bluff Point, 89, 95, 118, 201

Boomhower, A. D., 79
Boquet, 199
Boston, Mass., 51, 65, 67
Bowen, Shepard, 49
British, 12, 14, 17
Broadwell, Mary, 52
Broadwell family, 33
Bryce, Ambassador James, 116-17
Burgoyne, Gen. John, 14, 17
Burlington, Vt., 89
business & industry, 31, 35, 49, 51, 67, 79-80, 95, 97, 114-15, 141, 168, 183, 193-94, 201

C
Cady, Daniel L., 117
Cady, Heman, 79
Cadyville, 51
Canada, 11-12, 14, 17, 20, 22, 24-25, 31-32, 53-54
Canada Trade Act, 31
Canadian & Nova Scotia Refugee Tract, 17
Cannon Corners, 80
Capehart, Sen. Homer, 199
Carnes, William & Fred, 141
Catholic Summer School, 81, 90, 93, 166
Chaplain, Samuel de, 11, 115-16
Champlain, town of, 12, 17, 20, 22, 24-25, 31-33, 40, 47, 52, 79, 137, 163, 167-68, 199, 201
Champlain Canal, 32, 35
Chaplain College, 199
Champlain Transportation Co., 51, 65
Charlottesboro, 12
Chateaugay, town of, 40
Chateaugay R., 24
Chazy, Capt. de, 12
Chazy, town of, 12, 14, 20, 22, 25, 32, 40, 47, 67, 79, 113-15, 204

Chazy Lake, 199
Chazy (Saxe's) Landing, 17, 20, 22, 24, 32, 115
churches, 38-39, 53, 95, 115, 182
Civil War, 52-54
Clayburgh, 49, 199
Cliff Haven, 12, 90, 93, 116
Clinton, Gov. George, 20, 40
Clinton, town of, 17, 20
Clinton Community College, 201
Clintonville, 49, 52
Clinton Co. Agricultural Society, 32
Clinton Co. Council of the Arts, 202
Clinton Co. Fairgrounds, 79
Clinton Co. Historical Association, 12, 35, 202, 204
Clinton Co. Medical Society, 22
Clinton Co. Powder Works, 79
Clinton Co. Temperance Society, 35
Clinton Prison, 35, 38
clubs, 89, 167
commemorations, historical, 115-18, 137
Conway, Thomas F., 67, 137, 182
Cook, Gershom, 35
Cook, Ransom, 35
Cooperville, 17
Corbeau, 17
Corning, Charles W., 35
Crab Island, 202
Crown Point, 12, 14
Culver, Francis, 20
Cumberland Head, 12, 14, 17, 20, 22, 24, 32, 202
Cummings, Minnie, 111

D
Dannemora, 17, 20, 35, 38, 40, 47, 67
Dean, Elkanah, 14

Dearborn, Gen. Henry, 22
Delaware & Hudson Co., 65 80-81, 89
Delord, Henry, 22, 53
Delord, Frances, 31
Dewey, Elias, 22, 33
Dickens, Charles, 51
Dickinson, Sec. of War Jacob M., 116
Dodge, Daniel, 49
Dutchess Co., 17, 39
Dutchman's Point, 22

E
Eager, Margaret M., 137
East Beekmantown, 22, 52
Ellenburg, 17, 199
Ellis, Loren, 51
entertainment, 67, 93, 111, 141, 165-67, 182, 202-3
Erie Canal, 51
Essex Co., 12, 20, 47, 52, 199
Expo, 201

F
ferries, 20, 65, 115, 202
Ferrona, 49
fire companies, 96-97
fires, 47, 80-81, 118, 137, 167
Fisher, Cornelius, 53
Fisher, Forres, 53
Fishkill, 17
Fletcher, Aaron Dean, 52
Forest, 52
forts, 12, 24, 25, 53, 137
Franklin Co., 20, 24, 53
Fredenburg, Charles de, 12, 14, 17
French, 11, 12, 14
French, J. H., 52
Fresburg, 12
Fugitive Slave Act, 39

G
Getman, Carl B., 182
Gilbert, Dr. D. K., 79
Gilliland, William, 12
Goshen, 20
Grand Isle, Vt., 202
Graves, Mark, 17
Great Chazy R., 12, 24
Great Depression, 163, 168, 181-82
Great Lakes, 51
Great Northern R.R., 51-52
Green, Israel, 22, 25

H
Hale, Helen, 165
Hall, Rev. Frank, 53
Hallock Hill, 20, 22
Hampton, Gen. Wade, 24
Harrigan Corners, 199
Harrison, Pres. Benjamin, 89
Hay, William, 12
Hobart, Vice Pres. Garret A., 89
Holden, Fox, 81
hospitals, 114, 118, 138, 204-5
hotels, inn, taverns, 22, 25, 47, 65, 81, 89, 118, 166, 181, 183, 201
Howell, William T., 89
Howells, William Dean, 89
Hubbell, Julius C., 25
Hudson, Charles F., 79, 141
Hudson R., 14, 17, 20
Hughes, Gov. Charles E., 93, 116

I
Indians, 11, 12, 116
Ingraham, 22
iron industry, 49, 51, 67
Irona, 51-52
Isle La Motte, 12, 20, 115
Izard, Gen. George, 24-25

J
Janesboro, 12
Jay's Treaty, 22
Jefferson, Pres. Thomas, 22
Jericho, 20
Jerusalem, 20
Johnson, Corydon, 81, 182
Jusserand, Ambassador J. J., 93, 116-17

K
Keese, William, 39
Keeseville, 20, 49, 52
Kellogg, Dr. David, 67, 204
Kent-Dolord House, 114, 204
Kilmer, Joyce, 93
Knapp, Abel & Maria, 33
Knapp, Wallace, 114
Ku Klux Klan, 167-68

L
Lacolle, Que., 24
LaFramboise, Jean, 12
Lake Alice, 113
Lake Champlain, 11-12, 14, 17, 20, 22, 31-32, 52, 201-2
Lake Champlain Transportation Company, 202
Lake George, 12
Lake Ontario, 22
Lake Placid, 167
Lake Vermont, 11
land grants, 12-14, 17
Larkin, O. T., 79
LaRocque, Dr. Joseph H., 67, 204
Lawrence, William, 32
Lemieux, Postmaster General Rodolphe, 116-17
Levy brothers, 95
libraries, 33, 52, 89, 165, 181, 204
Lincoln, Pres. Abraham, 53
Little Chazy R., 12, 17
Loon Lake, 89
Lozier Company, 111

lumber industry, 31, 32, 51, 67
Lyon Mountain, 65, 67

M
Macdonough, Lt. Thomas, 24, 137
Macdonough monument, 202
Macomb, Gen. Alexander, 24-25, 137
Malone, 81, 111, 137
Mayor's Cup, 202
McKinley, Pres. William, 89, 93, 201
McLellan, Hugh, 116
Merkel, Isaac, 95
military maneuvers, 183
Miner, Alice T., 114
Miner, William H., 113, 204
Miner Agricultural Institute, 114
Miner Foundation, 113
missile silos, 199-200
Moffitt, Stephen, 54
Moffitsville, 49, 51
Monroe, Pres. James, 40
Montreal, Que., 20, 22, 24, 51-52, 65, 201
Mooers, Gen. Benjamin, 17, 20, 22
Mooers, town of, 17, 20, 32-33, 52-53, 67, 79-80, 95, 114, 163, 199
Mooers Camp Meeting Assoc., 115
Mooers Forks, 80, 115
Mooers Junction, 52
Moore, Sir Henry, 14
Moore, Pliny, 17, 22, 31, 137
Morgan, J. Pierpont, 65
Morrisonville, 52
Murray, Lt. Col. John, 22
museums, 114, 204
music, 79, 141, 202-3

N
Nash, Leo, 182
National Banking Act, 51
New Dean, agencies of, 181-82
New Military Tract, 17
newspapers, 22, 33, 40, 52, 118, 182, 199-200
New Sweden, 20, 49
New York City, 14, 32, 111, 113
New York State, 14, 17, 199, 202
Nilson, John, 111
North Hero, Vt., 22
Northway, 201
Norton, Christopher, 51
Nova Scotia, 17
Noyes, H. Otis, 182

O
O'Brien, J. F., 81
O'Brien, M. H., 67
Ogdensburg, 32, 40, 51-52, 67
Old Military Tract, 17
Olyphant, Talbot, 67
Otter Creek, Vt., 24

P
Palmer, Frank, 67
Palmer, John, 20
Palmer, Peter Sailly, 52
Palmer Hill, 49
Paris, Treaty of, 12
Payette-Mendelsohn Company, 95
Peru, 12, 17, 20, 22, 40, 47, 49, 52, 67, 79, 166, 183
Petersburgh, 49
Pickett, Edmund, 49
Pickett's Corners, 49
Pike, Col. Zebulon, 22
Pike's Cantonment, 22, 137
Platt, Charles, 20
Platt, Levi & Eliza, 33
Platt, Moss Kent, 49
Platt, Theodorus, 20
Platt, Zephaniah, 17
Plattsburgh, 11-12, 20, 22, 24-25, 32-33, 40, 47, 49, 51-54, 65, 67, 79-81, 93, 95-97, 111, 116, 137, 166-67, 182-83, 199-201
Plattsburgh Air Force Base, 199-200
Plattsburgh & Montreal R.R., 52
Plattsburgh Barracks, 53, 116-17, 137, 165, 199
"Plattsburgh Idea," 137-38
Plattsburgh State Normal School, 81
Plattsburgh State University, 81, 200-1, 203
Pleistocene Age, 11
Point au Fer, 12, 14, 22
Point au Roche, 12, 14, 35, 201
police departments, 97
Pope, John Russell, 141
Port Henry, 51
Port Jackson, 32
Port Kent, 52
Powers, Asahel Lynde, 33
Prescott, Rufus, 49
Prevost, Gov. Gen. George, 25
Pring, Capt. Daniel, 24

Q
Quakers, 20, 22
Quebec Act, 14
Quebec City, 90
Quebec Province, 115, 201

R
railroads, 40, 49, 51-52, 65, 67
Ransom, Jabez, 22
Redford, 35, 49
Redford Crown Glass Company, 35
Richards, Rev. N., 89
Richelieu R., 20, 32
roads, 20, 22, 40, 49, 51, 67, 201
Rockefeller, Gov. Nelson, 200
Rogers, J. & J. Company, 49, 67, 97, 115

Roosevelt, Franklin D., 137, 181
Roosevelt, Theodore, 93, 137-38
Root, Sen. Elihu, 117
Rouses Point, 17, 20, 22, 24-25, 33, 40, 51-52, 65, 67, 79, 93, 96, 111, 137, 163, 183, 202
Russia (NY), 20, 49

S
Sackets Harbor, 24
Sailly, F. L. C., 35
Sailly, Peter, 31
St. Albans, Vt., 54
St. John, Que., 32, 51
St. Lawrence Co., 53
St. Lawrence R., 11
Salmon R., 12
Sampson, Lester, 22, 47
Saranac, town of, 17, 20, 47, 49, 111
Saranac Lake, 51, 167
Saranac R., 12, 17, 20, 22, 24-25, 31, 35, 49, 51-52, 79, 116-18
Saxe, Matthew, 22, 32
Scheier, Isaiah, 95
Scheier, Joel, 181
schools & colleges, 22, 32, 40-41, 52, 79-81, 90, 113-14, 199-200
Schuyler Falls, 20, 47, 183
Scott, Alexander, 22, 25
ships, 20, 32, 51, 65, 90, 115-16
Shute, Ruth & Samuel, 33
Signor, James H., 49
Silver, Dr. Cassius, 204
Sing Sing, 35
Skinner, St. John B. L., 35
Smith, Gov. Alfred E., 114, 181
Smith, Frank F., 67
Smith, Levi, 17
Smith, Loyal F., 140-41
Smith, Stephen Keese, 39
Smith & Graves patent, 17
Sousa, John Philip, 93

Sperry, Gilead, 22
Standish, 65, 67
Stetson, Francis Lynde, 137
Stower, James N., 67
Strack, Shirley, 181
Sugarbush, 199
Swanton, Vt., 199
Swastica, 20
Sweet, William, 115

T
Taft, Pres. William H., 93, 116-17, 201
Taylor, Bushrod S., 115
Tefft, H. & O. A., 51
telephones, 79, 114, 165
temperance & prohibition, 35, 163, 181-82
Ticonderoga, 11-12, 14, 17, 65, 89
tourism, 95, 201
Tredwell, Thomas, 38
trolley lines, 80-81, 182
Tuthill, A. G. D., 33

U
underground railroad, 40, 53
Union, The, 20, 22, 32, 39

V
Valcour, 12, 14, 166, 202
Vanderbilt, Cornelius, 65
Vermont, 11, 17, 20, 22, 24, 79, 115, 199, 202
Vert, Charles J., 137
Vilas Home, 96
Volstead Act, 163

W
Walworth, Chancellor Reuben, 35
War of 1812, 22, 24-25, 38
Warren Co., 47
Washington Co., 20, 31

Watson, Thomas B., 32
Watson, Winslow C., 52
WCTU, 182
Weed, Smith M., 65, 67, 93, 97
West Chazy, 52
Western Union Telegraph Company, 65
Whitehall, 14, 32, 51, 65
Wilkinson, Gen. James, 24
Williams, Andrew, 49
Williamsburgh, 49
Willsboro, 138, 167, 199
Wilson, Pres. Woodrow, 163
WMFF, 181
Wood, Amasa, 67
Wood, Col. Leonard, 137-38
Wood, Wallace, 67
Wood's Falls, 67, 80
Woolsey, Melancton, 20
World War I, 137-38
World War II, 193, 199
YMCA, 95, 140

ABOUT THE AUTHORS

Carol Bedore
Mary Leggett   Allan Everest
Helen Allan

Helen W. Allan has chaired the Clinton County Bicentennial Committee's publications subcommittee during two years of planning for the county's 200th birthday. She has been director of the Clinton County Historical Association and curator of the County Museum since 1973. She also edits *North Country Notes,* the Historical Association's monthly publication. In 1987 she wrote *Clinton Prison at Dannemora,* and has contributed to *Naho* and *The Conservationist.*

Carol Getman Bedore is the Head of Acquisitions and a library consultant at the Clinton-Essex-Franklin Library System. She has written articles which have appeared in several publications. Ms. Bedore is a member of the Bicentennial Committee and its publications group.

Allan S. Everest is a native of Vermont, a veteran of World War II, and has graduate degrees from Columbia University. He has resided in Clinton County since 1947. He is retired after thirty-six years of teaching at State University of New York, Plattsburgh, where he taught American and New York history. Dr. Everest is the author of ten books of regional history including volumes on historic architecture, rum-running, and the War of 1812.

Mary G. Leggett was a consultant for the Clinton-Essex-Franklin Library System for twenty-three years. She was editor of *The Trailblazer,* the newsletter for the library system for over twenty years. *York State Tradition, The N.Y.S. Bookmark* and *Christian Science Monitor* have published her writings. Also a member of Clinton County's Bicentennial Committee, Ms. Leggett was the author of the Town of Plattsburgh's 1985 bicentennial pageant. She currently edits the town of Plattsburgh's *Quarterly Bulletin.*

The Shepard P. Bowen house was at 22 Macomb Street in Plattsburgh. History of Clinton and Franklin Counties, New York, *D. H. Hurd*